LINGUISTIC
THEORY
AND
LANGUAGE
DESCRIPTION

LINGUISTIC THEORY AND LANGUAGE DESCRIPTION

Carol M. Eastman
University of Washington

Edgar V. Winans
Series Editor

J. B. Lippincott Company
Philadelphia
New York   San Jose   Toronto

ISBN 0-397-47378-8

Library of Congress Catalog Card Number 77-29170

Printed in the United States of America

2 4 6 8 9 7 5 3 1

Library of Congress Cataloging in Publication Data

Library of Congress Cataloging in Publication Data

Eastman, Carol M
    Linguistic theory and language description.

    Bibliography: p.
    Includes index.
    1.   Linguistics.   2.   Linguistic analysis (Linguistics).
I.   Title.
P121.E2   410   77-29170
ISBN 0-397-47378-8

Preface

This book, intended for courses in both linguistics and anthropological linguistics, deals with the distinction made between the two fields since the late 1950s and 1960s. Today, what is usually called linguistics is the domain of linguistics departments, while earlier in this century the field of linguistics was considered a part of anthropology.

This book emphasizes that there are two distinct goals for the scientific study of language: One is an outgrowth of American descriptive linguistics which dominated the field from 1933 to 1957; the other took a different direction arising from pre-1933 American linguistics and took advantage of recent innovations in other fields such as philosophy, psychology and mathematics. Both approaches to the study of language are modern and productive. Linguistics aims to make explicit the nature of language and the process of language acquisition. Anthropological linguistics aims to describe and compare languages and to pursue the relationship of language and culture.

I wish to express my gratitude to Douglas Paterson, Elizabeth Edwards and Maxine Schmidt for reading the manuscript in its roughest form and for their constructive comments and criticisms. Maxine Schmidt submitted some of the questions at the end of each chapter. I am also indebted to Edgar V. Winans and to Richard Heffron of J. B. Lippincott Company for their help and to Nancy Roma for preparing the manuscript.

Contents

ꟼntrόduction

Bloomfield (1933) defines linguistics as the science of the study of language. Today this definition covers many endeavors. Broadly speaking, it includes language teaching and most of what is known now as speech science. However, it is generally thought that today's linguist is concerned primarily with describing language use and with describing the nature of language.

Although the approaches to each of these tasks have different goals, methods and theories, they both evolved from a common background in the scientific linguistics presented by Bloomfield and developed from nineteenth-century origins.

The division of the endeavors of the linguist into language description (the description of language use) and linguistic theory (the description of the nature of language) is an arbitrary one. However, since 1957 when Noam Chomsky published his *Syntactic Structures*, many linguists have tended to divide into these camps. Adherents of Chomsky argue that, because of a "revolution" in linguistics, the goals of linguistics are to be seen in explaining the language acquisition process by developing and testing a theory of what knowledge underlies the acquisition of language. In their view, those who describe languages from samples of language use are *not* linguists, in the sense that their concern is not with the nature of language but rather with language as behavior. Persons concerned with the nature of language and the process of language acquisition feel that, once they understand both the innate and acquired knowledge which allows for language acquisition, they then, as linguists, may focus on the description of language use as it relates to the linguistic knowledge humans have.

Meanwhile, many students who continue to concern themselves with language use generally call themselves linguists, but often with qualifying terms. Among those who focus on language use are anthropological linguists, psycholinguists, sociolinguists, structural linguists and descriptive linguists. They engage in *language description.*

Other linguists tend to adopt labels which reflect the particular aspect of the nature and acquisition of linguistic knowledge which interests them, calling themselves generative phonologists, transformational grammarians, syntacticians or generative semanticists. Occasionally they debate the merits of such positions as the transformationalist versus the lexicalist viewpoint regarding a particular theoretical approach. These people engage primarily in *linguistics.*

The situation is much as it was when descriptive linguistics was the dominant paradigm of linguistics with various people specializing as phonemicists and morphologists. Disputes would develop between scholars advocating item and process descriptions of data over item and arrangement ones, or between proponents and opponents of the notion of the "psychological reality" of the phoneme (see Chapter One). Rather than argue the theory and method of linguistic description as do the linguists, scholars dealing with descriptions of language now use descriptive methods and techniques for observing and describing languages in relation to speech and communicative behavior.

By no means are the people engaged in language description any more linguists than those who focus on theory. The point is that, despite the common origins of American linguistics, two fundamentally separate tasks now capture the attention of linguists. Each endeavor holds that eventually linguistics will be able to account for language use and language acquisition, as well as explain the nature of language as a cognitive ability. *Linguistic Theory and Language Description* is an examination of some of the issues involved in both tasks.

In Chapter One we examine the development of linguistics as a science designed with a theory and method for discovering the units which combine in speech. We see how language is viewed as being composed of levels which could be analyzed separately with the resulting description of all the levels seen as a grammar. The grammar is a description of the speech of a representative speaker of the language.

In Chapter Two the idea that language is something more abstract than speech is developed. To describe speech is to get at language as it is used. The advent of structuralism brought to linguistics the idea that a grammar might otherwise be seen as a description of what speakers of a language know about their language – that is, what the system of language is – that underlies speech.

The concepts presented in Chapters One and Two are the bases for the ideas presented in the rest of the book. Chapter One provides the idea of language use as describable. This idea is the basis for the various models of grammatical description explicated in Chapter Four, where we also see examples of the work done by people who see language as knowledge which needs to be characterized in order to understand and describe how the knowledge is used.

Chapter Three emphasizes the concerns of language scholars with respect to the criteria necessary for evaluating the results of their work. Descriptions of language use strive to meet certain criteria, and formal models of the nature of language strive to meet others.

The final chapter reviews the most current questions being addressed by scholars dealing with language use (animal communication and sociolinguistics) and those dealing with language as knowledge (psycholinguistics, child language acquisition and artificial intelligence).

Throughout the book the reader is encouraged to note the various implicit definitions of language that guide the types of study done. Language is variously viewed as speech, communication and knowledge (cognition). Whatever the definition, language scholars share an ultimate interest in describing and accounting for the interrelatedness of thinking and speaking. It is hoped that this book will show the range of approaches to linguistic theory and language description available for pursuing this interest.

ONE

Descriptive Linguistics

Development and Goals of Descriptive Linguistics

DESCRIPTIVE LINGUISTICS deals chiefly with languages at particular points in time rather than throughout their historical development. Usually considered a behavioral science, it is also concerned with language as a phenomenon. It emerged in the twentieth century as a challenge to the goals and methodology of nineteenth-century linguists.

Linguistics as a field of study is hardly two hundred years old. In 1786 Sir William Jones, an English jurist and scholar, uncovered the genetic relations among certain languages. Through the Asiatic Society of Bengal, which he founded while serving as a supreme court judge in India, he promoted, among other interests, the idea that Sanskrit, the classical language of ancient India, stemmed from the same source as Latin and Greek.

During the nineteenth century, European linguists built

upon Jones's ideas and findings. Through the comparison of language structures they established the Indo-European family by using Sanskrit and other classical languages in tracing the interrelationships of various European languages. Linguists firmly grounded in their "systematic, rational analysis of the forms of speech" (Pedersen 1949: 12) produced grammars that tried to fit their broad range of linguistic data into the structure of the Indo-European model. Most studies were of languages having a written record and "belonging" to the Indo-European family.

At the beginning of the twentieth century, Franz Boas, a German-born anthropologist, challenged the conventional method and technique of studying and describing *all* languages. What of languages having no written records and no ties with the Indo-European family? The American Indian languages, having no written records and no such ties, were a glaring example. Boas's earlier geographical research on the Central Eskimos of Baffin Island had convinced him that an accurate and objective description of any people required an accurate and objective knowledge of their culture. To substantiate this conclusion further and to underscore the shortcomings of the Indo-European model, he began gathering information on American Indian languages and eventually developed a method for describing languages by using native speakers in their cultural milieu. *Handbook of American Indian Languages* (1911), the culmination of the fieldwork of Boas and his students, not only laid the foundations for the science of descriptive linguistics, but spurred the development of a method that emphasized rigorous analysis of speech data.

To Boas, language as the subject matter of linguistics was confined to human speech, composed of a limited number of sounds per language grouped together with fixed meanings used to communicate ideas. A uniform method of analysis supposedly used for each language described in the *Handbook* showed that *not* all languages share many of the fundamental features of Indo-European languages (such as case endings and certain tenses) and that the Indo-European model was of little value in describing the languages of North American Indians.

In the course of the development of the method, discovery

procedures for eliciting speech data and yielding analyses of it were devised and refined. We shall now consider the basic discovery procedures.

Phonetics

ARTICULATORY PHONETICS, the basis of Boas's methodology, is the study of speech sounds with regard to how they are produced by the speech organs. For descriptive linguists it is the logical starting point for describing speech. As Dinneen (1967: 7) notes:

> By regarding language primarily as sound the linguist can take advantage of the fact that all human beings produce speech sounds with essentially the same equipment. While the sounds of foreign languages may sound strange or difficult to us, all of them can be described with reasonable accuracy by accounting for the movements of the articulatory organs that produce them.

Boas (1911:35) believed that three points had to be considered in discussing languages objectively: the constituent phonetic elements of the language, the clusters of ideas expressed by phonetic groups, and the methods of combining and modifying phonetic groups.

Transcribing sample utterances from a native informant's speech is a descriptive linguist's first task. Here articulatory phonetics becomes invaluable. Linguists use a number of transcription systems. These systems consist of symbols that represent the speaker's articulations. Since the object is a description of speech, the linguist must imitate the speech and describe it according to its POINT and MANNER OF ARTICULATION. It is important to know whether or not the LARYNX, which contains the VOCAL CORDS, helped to produce the sound. If there is vocal-cord vibration, the sound is VOICED; if there is not, it is VOICELESS.

The manner and the point of articulation — the main axes of speech production — usually form the basis of a phonetic chart; usually the former is the vertical axis and the latter the horizontal axis. Voice is classified as a subcategory of the manner of articulation.

Figure 1–1. *Phonetic Chart* (with examples of common English consonants)

Manner of Articulation		Point of Articulation			
		Bilabial	*Labiodental*	*Alveolar*	*Velar*
Stop	v/less	p		t	k
	voiced	b		d	g
Fricative	v/less		f		
	voiced		v		
Nasal	voiced	m		n	ŋ

Most phonetic transcription systems use symbols for the sounds which form the intersection of various points and manners of articulation on the chart. In Figure 1–1, regular English consonant letters symbolize the intersections for all but the sound classified as a voiced velar nasal. English orthography lacks a single symbol for the sound which is the *ng* as in *sing.* Phonetically that sound may be represented by [ŋ]. (Note that, by convention, all phonetic symbols are represented in square brackets to distinguish them from ordinary letters of the alphabet.)

Boas developed a system of transcription for the Bureau of American Ethnology and that system is used to transcribe the data for all the languages described by him and his students in the *Handbook of American Indian Languages.* But today descriptive linguists use a transcription system known as the International Phonetic Alphabet (IPA), which originated in the last half of the nineteenth century and achieved its final form in the early part of the twentieth (Figure 1–2).

In transcribing speech sounds a single symbol should be used for each sound transcribed and that symbol should be employed consistently for that sound. For example, [ŋ] should be used to transcribe the final sound in *sing.* If both the symbols [n] and [g] were used, it would not be possible to distinguish *singer* [sIŋɚ] from *finger* [fIŋgɚ] in data representing speakers who pronounce the medial consonants in those words differently. The same distinction across word boundaries is obscured if two symbols [ng] are used for [ŋ]. In other words, consider

Consonants	Bilabial.	Labiedental.	Dental and lveolar.	Retroflex.	Palato-alveolar.	Alveolo-palatal.	Palatal.	Velar.	Uvular.	Pharyngal.	Glottal.
Plasive . . .	p b		t d	t ḍ			c ɟ	k g	q ɑ		ʔ
Nasal . . .	m	m	n	ŋ			ɲ	ŋ	N		
Lateral . . .			l	ɭ			ʎ				
" fricative .			ɬ h								
Rolled . . .			r						R		
Flapped . .			r	r					R		
Rolled fricative .			ɼ								
Fricative . . .	Φ β	f v	θð|sz|ɹ	ʂ ʐ	ʃ ʒ	ç ʑ	ç j	x ɣ	χ ʁ	ħ ʕ	h ɦ
Frictionless Continu-ants and Semi-vowels . .	w|ɥ	ʋ	ɹ				j (ɥ)	(w) y			

Vowels	Rounded						Front Center Back				
Close . . .	(y ʉ u)						i y ɨ ʉ ɯ u				
Half-close . .	(ø o)						e ø ə ɤ o				
Half-open . .	(œ ɔ)						ɛ ɜ ɐ ʌ ɔ				
							æ ɐ				
Open . . .	(ɒ)						a ɑ ɒ				

Figure 1–2. The International Phonetic Alphabet (from The Principles of the International Phonetic Association, 1949:10).

ongoing versus the phrase *long owing. Ongoing* is [aŋgo(w)iŋ] where both the [n] and [g] are distinct sounds in the first part of the word and *long owing* is [lɔŋo(w)Iŋ] where [ŋ] represents the single sound heard at the end of the first word. Two factors determine the choice of symbol for a particular sound: the transcriber's knowledge of articulatory phonetics, and the symbols used for each intersection of point and manner of articulation according to the IPA.

Once a sufficient body of speech data has been transcribed such that the linguist may assume to have recorded every sound in that particular language, then a phonetic chart for that language becomes the next task.

Fortunately for English-speaking students, many IPA symbols are the symbols used in writing. However, spelling should not be solely relied on because English spelling often uses more than one symbol for a single sound. For example, gh, in English spelling represents many different phonetic elements, none of which resembles the point and manner of articulation of phonetic [g] or [h]. Consider the following:

ENGLISH SPELLING	PHONETIC TRANSCRIPTION
through	[ɵru]
enough	[inəf]
bough	[bau]
cough	[kɔf]
dough	[dow]
thigh	[ɵai]

As may be seen from Figure 1–2, consonants differ from vowels in their possible articulatory definitions. For American English consonants some of the major points of articulation are as follows:

BILABIAL — contact is made with both lips — [p] [b] [m]

LABIODENTAL — contact made at lower lip by upper teeth — [f] [v]

DENTAL — contact made by tongue at upper teeth — [t] [d] [n] (some speakers)

ALVEOLAR — contact made by tongue behind the upper teeth at the roof of the mouth — [t] [d] [n] (most speakers)

ALVEO-PALATAL — contact made by tongue further back toward the palate — [š] OR [s] as in *shin* and [ž] or [ʒ] as in *garage* or *beige* or *azure*

PALATAL — contact made by tongue at hard palate — [č] or [ts] as in *chin*, [ǰ] or [dʒ] as in *gin*

The symbols [s], [ʒ], [ts], and [dʒ] are used less frequently than [š], [ž], [č], and [v] respectively. Generally if a transcriber uses [s] and [ʒ], consistency requires [ts] and [dʒ]. However, for typographical convenience and for adherence to the ideal of using single symbols, the "checked" series is preferred.

VELAR — contact made by tongue further back than the hard palate — [k] as in *cake* and [g] as in *gate*

GLOTTAL — closure and opening of the vocal cords — [ʔ as in [bəʔn̩] pronounced without an alveolar stop as opposed to [bətn̩] for *button*. This is common in the speech of some New Englanders.

NASAL — the air flowing through the nose (nasal cavity) rather than the mouth (oral cavity) — [m] [n] [ŋ]

LATERAL — the sound is produced by placing the articulator (e.g., the tongue) at the side of the oral cavity — [l]

ROLLED — the tongue is rolled (gently — not rapidly trilled or flapped as in the French "r" Americans have such trouble with) as it makes contact with the point of articulation (in English the point of articulation is the alveolar ridge) — [r] as in *run*

FRICATIVE — the air flow is temporarily restricted as it passes through the oral cavity causing a "noise" or friction — [ð] as in *that* and [θ] as in *thin*, [s] as in *sin*, and [z] as in *zero*

It should be noticed that phonetic charts for consonants, with respect to the point where articulation occurs, move from the front of the mouth (upper left of the chart) at the lips (bilabial) to the back of the mouth (upper right of the chart) at the glottis.

The points of articulation for vowels are labeled *front* (when the tongue is at the front of the mouth), *central* (the tongue is at the center of the mouth), and *back*.

Symbols for vowels may be arranged according to their point and manner of articulation so as to reflect the structure of the oral cavity where articulation occurs. Vowel articulation is concerned with the height of the tongue in the mouth and with the correlative jaw position as *high, mid,* or *low*. To demonstrate this, place your chin in your hand and pronounce the vowels: for high vowels the jaw will be high; for low vowels the position of the jaw will be lowered.

		Front	Central	Back
High	tense	i	i	u
	lax	I		U
Mid	tense	e	ə	o
	lax	ε		ɔ
		æ		
Low			a	

To define a vowel articulatorily, one would say [i] is a high-front tense vowel, and [ɔ] is a mid-low back-lax vowel. TENSE and LAX refer to degrees of tenseness or stricture of the muscles of the articulator's tongue. If the muscles are tensed, the vowel is tense; if they are relaxed, it is lax.

A further dimension, ROUNDNESS is important in pronouncing English vowels. This dimension refers to the rounding of the lips and is particularly important with back vowels. The high-back tense [u] is rounded, while the mid-back tense [o] is less rounded, and the lower-back lax [ɔ] is weakly rounded. If you say the words [but] boot, [bot] *boat,* and [bɔt] *bought* while looking in a mirror, you can see the shape of your lips reveal degrees of rounding. In contrast, the other English vowels are unrounded.

Again, the symbols differ from conventional spelling usage and more symbols are added because more vowels are articulated than are written. Consider the following examples.

English Spelling	Phonetic Transcription
beet	[bit]
bit	[bɪt]
bait	[bet]
bet	[bɛt]
bat	[bæt]
boot	[but]
put	[pUt]
bought	[bɔt]
bought	[bat] (rare, used by speakers in the Midland speech area)
boat	[bot]
but	[bət]
just	[jɨst] (as in "just a minute" spoken rapidly)

Many of the symbols which are unlike conventional orthographic symbols have special names such as [ə] 'schwa,' [ð] *eth*, and [æ] *ash*. Here is where the descriptive linguist begins a description of a language by transcribing what sounds a native speaker articulates in speech, using a system with symbols for how and where the sounds are made.

Thus, a chart of the symbols for *all* the sounds used by speakers is the first part of any language description. When enough data have been transcribed so that all possible articulated sounds have been noted, all the sounds are tabulated. The linguist now has a body of data and can proceed to the next level of description of the speech sample.

Phonetic Diacritics and Suprasegmentals

The requirement that *all* of the sounds used by speakers need to be described and transcribed has some implications beyond what has just been discussed. Although the next level of description may be begun once the sounds in the body of data are transcribed, some facts about the nature of a complete phonetic transcription should be considered. Speech, although composed of isolatable sounds, is also shaped by features peculiar to the sounds as they occur in combination. These features are called SUPRASEGMENTALS. They are features of sound that cannot properly be considered unitary segments. Length, stress, and tone are suprasegmental phenomena "because of the practice of writing them phonetically by means of marks made above the symbols indicating segments." (Langacker 1968: 151.)

There are special symbols used in a phonetic transcription to indicate suprasegmentals. A phonetic transcription requires, as well, a means of distinguishing from each other segments of speech which are larger than the isolatable sounds. That is, in speech, there are sound properties of syllables or groups of sounds which need to be transcribed. We will see that consonants and vowels which are perceived as relatively longer than others may be noted by using the symbol ♦ after the sound. Thus, in English we can indicate that the vowels in *hide* and *height* are the same in point and manner of articulation but differ in length. For example [hai♦d] "hide," [hait] "height." The length noted is a suprasegmental feature of the syllable.

Other properties of syllables and groups of sounds have to do with their perceived stress and pitch. Some common symbols for stress are (´) PRIMARY, (^) SECONDARY, (ˇ) WEAK and (`) TERTIARY. Primary and tertiary stress occur in the English words *dictionary* and *animation* (Gleason 1961:42). Thus, [dIkšənèri] and [ǽnIméšən]. Weak stress often alternates in variants of a single word. Gleason uses the example of *contents* which may be pronounced either [kóntènts] or [kóntînts]. Stress is what distinguishes many nouns from verbs for some speakers of English. For example, *I* [pɜ˞mIt] *you to get a* [pɜ˞mIt]. The use of *bláck bîrd* is a classic illustration of secondary stress. The adjective-plus-noun combination "implies a bird that is described as black; the second a particular kind of bird, which, incidentally, may or may not be black. *That white bird is an albino bláckbìrd* makes sense if the stresses are as indicated, but no sense if we substitute *bláck bîrd*." (Gleason 1961:45)

Phonemics

Earlier in this chapter we discussed Boas's view that language description should describe the sounds of the language and then illustrate how the sounds are grouped together. However, Edward Sapir, one of his students, had other ideas that influenced the eventual codification of descriptive linguistics.

Sapir's approach to linguistic analysis, like that of his teacher, evolved from his studies on the ethnology of various Indian groups in the United States. In his *Language: An Introduction to the Study of Speech* (1921), Sapir introduced principles which became part and parcel of the methodology of descriptive linguistics. To him, language is a mixture of forms and concepts. His approach to the sounds of language and his part in the development of PHONEMICS illustrate this. For example, a PHONEME became "a functionally significant unit in the rigidly defined pattern of configuration of sounds peculiar to a language." (Sapir 1933:247) As such, it is differentiated from a PHONETIC ELEMENT (PHONE) defined as, "an objectively definable entity in the articulated and perceived totality of speech."

Prior to Sapir's studies, the word phoneme was used by some European linguists. But it was Sapir who advanced the idea that a speaker hears phonemes rather than phonetic elements. This notion arose from his work as a field linguist teaching native speakers to write down the actual sounds they used when they spoke. Frequently students would consistently write sounds other than what they actually spoke.

What occurred may be shown by an English example. If the word *pin* is spoken, its phonetic transcription – the written representation of what is actually articulated – would be more like [pʰIn] with an [ʰ] used as a diacritic representing the puff of air following the /p/. An English speaker, however, would be more likely to write *pin*, linking the initial sound of the word with the final sound in the English *sleep*. If asked what sound *pin* and *sleep* have in common, an English speaker would reply, unhesitatingly, /p/. Phonetically the words actually have no common element: the initial sound in *pin* is an aspirated [pʰ]; the final sound in *sleep* is an unaspirated [p]. What is shared in *pin* and *sleep* is a phoneme: the feeling is that there is a /p/ not a [pʰ] in *pin* just as in *sleep*.

According to Sapir, certain constraints in language prevent speakers from recognizing phonetic distinctions which deviate from the pattern for their language. For example, the sound pattern of English is such that *pin* has the same sound initially as *sleep* does finally and as *happen* does medially. A speaker of another language might hear two or three different sounds when the English speaker utters the English [p].

Describing a language requires more than a description of the sounds that are articulated in it. The linguist must describe what the native speaker *hears* as well as *speaks*. However, the linguist/observer cannot hear a language as a native speaker does and consequently needs criteria for describing what sounds are phonemic amid all the sounds of the language (both segmental and suprasegmental) phonetically transcribed in the body of data. These criteria constitute the method of PHONEMIC ANALYSIS.

The basic assumption of this method is the definition of the phoneme. In general, Sapir's definition of it as "a functionally significant unit in the rigidly defined pattern of configuration of sounds peculiar to a language" still stands. The idea that the phoneme exists in a patterned way in the mind of a native speaker, however, did not lend itself to the development of a mechanical procedure for identifying such units in observable and recorded data. Yet, descriptive linguistics required a definition which would allow phonemes to be identified using mechanical discovery procedures. Since the patterned configuration referred to by Sapir could not be observed, the descriptive linguist objectified his notion in such a way that phonemes could be identified from a body of speech data. In contrast, structural linguistics focused on language as an abstract system as opposed to language as speech. In the structural approach, Sapir's definition of the phoneme also applied to and underlay the development of structuralist phonology. The idea that sounds exist in the minds of native speakers in relation to each other served as the foundation for structural linguistics. Ironically, Sapir himself was a descriptive linguist who rigorously applied the operational procedures and methods of the discipline even though his ideas later shifted the focus of linguistics from language as speech (*parole*) to language as an abstract system (*langue*).

According to Gleason (1961:261), a phoneme "is a class of sounds which 1) are phonetically similar and 2) show certain characteristic patterns of distribution in the language or dialect under consideration." The class of sounds defined as the phoneme may be in FREE VARIATION. For example, if you were to repeat the English word *tea* over and over again, the class of features or sounds in the initial /t/ might vary, but you would be still saying *tea*.

Whenever each class of sounds defined as a phoneme occurs in a context where other phonemes cannot occur, they are said to be in COMPLEMENTARY DISTRIBUTION. For example, in English where in *spin* the sound /p/ after /s/ is pronounced without a puff of air (is unaspirated) while in *pin* the initial /p/ is aspirated, an English speaker perceives that *spin* and *pin* both have the sound or phoneme /p/ even though the phonetic element heard is different, [p] versus [pʰ]. In English [p] and [pʰ] are in complementary distribution, aspirated /p/ never occurs after /s/. [p] and [pʰ] are called allophones of the phoneme /p/. Essentially, an ALLOPHONE of a phoneme is a class of sounds which occurs in complementary distribution or in free variation with respect to another class of sounds. (Note that, by convention, as phonetic elements are represented in square brackets, phonemic elements are represented in slashes.)

In English, [p] and [pʰ] never occur in the same environment. Where English speakers use [p] they do not use [pʰ]. When an English speaker says *pill* and *lip,* the p sounds are actually phonetically different although most speakers think they are both *p*s. In *pill* the initial sound is [pʰ]; in *lip* the final sound is [p]. The fact of variants of phonetically similar sounds occurring in mutually exclusive environments exemplifies the notion of complementary distribution. Likewise, no English speaker pronounces *spin* as [spʰIn] or *pin* as [pIn]. *Pin* is [pʰIn] and *spin* is [spIn]. The [pʰ] variant of /p/ occurs in the initial position in English and is in complementary distribution with the other allophones of the phoneme. When variants of a sound occur in the same environment and it makes no difference in the language, the sounds are in free variation. In English, /t/ may be pronounced either with the dental or alveolar position as its point of articulation. Thus, [t] dental *t* and [t] alveolar *t* are in free variation in English.

A descriptive statement of a language begins with what is known as PHONEMIC ANALYSIS. Such an analysis is essentially a process whereby a phonetic transcription is refined mechanically so that it will represent the "significant" sounds of the language.

Here are the steps in a phonemic analysis.

Phonetics	Gather a body of speech data and transcribe it, using the International Phonetic Alphabet.
	Tabulate all the sounds in the data according to their point and manner of articulation.
Phonemics	List suspicious pairs. That is, "pairs of sounds which seem to be phonetically similar [to each other] and hence possible allophones of the same phoneme" (Gleason 1961:275). Thus, [p] and [b] might be listed as a suspicious pair since they have the same point and manner of articulation.
	Frame a generalizing hypothesis. If [p] and [b] are in complementary distribution, perhaps [t] and [d] are as well.
	Test the hypothesis by tabulating the distribution of each sound in a suspicious pair. If [t] and [d] may be shown to occur in the same environment, and a native speaker distinguishes them, they belong to separate phonemes—*tot* and *dot, got* and *god, utter* and *udder*.

A phonemic transcription presents a body of data composed of sounds distinguished by a native speaker. A /p/ phoneme in a particular language, however, does not necessarily represent the same class of sounds as a /p/ in another language. It must be remembered that phonemes are to be seen as points in the structure of a particular language. Hence, Gleason's operational definition is restricted in its application to a single language.

We should remember that the goal of descriptive linguistics is the development of uniform methods for describing languages so they could be compared with each other. The initial procedure developed for accomplishing this goal consists of isolating units that are language specific. We will see that the procedures for describing languages at successfully higher levels of description next involve analyzing groups of phonemes into minimal units of grammatical meaning (see the section on morphology) and then analyzing those units into minimal units of grammatical arrangement (see section on syntax).

Consequently, the methods of descriptive linguistics produced descriptions of individual languages in their own terms. Language descriptions on this model could not be compared to each other after all. Therefore, the goal of descriptive linguistics changed as it developed from facilitating language classification to the goal of providing *adequate* descriptions of individual languages as they differ from other languages rather than as they are similar to each other. (We shall deal with adequacy as a concept and a goal in linguistics in Chapter Three.)

Gleason's *Introduction to Descriptive Linguistics* (1961) in many ways constitutes *the* codification of descriptive linguistics. In it he ironically states:

> The first [task of descriptive linguistics] is to describe individual languages or dialects in terms of their own characteristic structure. For each of the numerous speech forms this is a separate task; the structure of no other language is directly relevant.

Moreover, "the classification of languages is not within the province of descriptive linguistics, though many descriptive linguists also work on this problem." (1961:440)

Even so, he maintains that descriptive linguistics would facilitate language classification:

> For every language and major dialect, there would be needed at least the following: a summary of the phonology and mor-

phology; a vocabulary of, say, several thousand words; a small body of recorded texts together with a translation into some better known language; a statement of where and by whom the language is spoken, and the name by which it is called by its speakers and the neighboring peoples. With this much information, a definitive listing and classification of languages could be made. (Gleason 1961:454)

Once the descriptive linguist has discovered the phonemes in a body of phonetically transcribed data, isolation of the minimal units of grammatical meaning becomes the next step in language description. This procedure is called morphology.

Morphology

According to Gleason (1961:53), the MORPHEME as a basic unit of linguistic expression is both "the smallest unit which is grammatically pertinent" and the smallest meaningful unit in the structure of language. Whereas phonemes are composed of phonetic material, morphemes are composed of phonemes.

As phonemes have variants called allophones, morphemes have variants known as ALLOMORPHS. An allomorph "is a variant of a morpheme which occurs in certain definable environments." (Gleason 1961:62) Allomorphs may be phonologically or morphologically conditioned. The morpheme "plural" in English is an example of a morpheme with both phonologically and morphologically conditioned allomorphs.

The *plural* morpheme is /s/ after voiceless stops (*cat, cats*), /z/ after vowels, voiced stops, liquids (l and r), glides (w and y) and nasals (*bed, beds; sofa, sofas; car, cars; cow, cows; bun, buns*) and /əz/ after affricates and sibilants (*witch, witches; nose, noses*). /s/, /z/, and /əz/ are phonologically conditioned allomorphs of the grammatical unit "plural" in English since the sounds they occur in association with determine which allomorphs will be used.

Child, children; goose, geese; shrimp, shrimp — these are also forms of the "plural" morpheme in English. Although not phonologically conditioned, these plural forms are still allomorphs because they are "plural". Such allomorphs are said to be morphologically conditioned.

Morphology is the technique employed by the descriptive linguist to discover the morphemes in a body of speech data. In many ways the method is analogous to that employed in phonemics. The basic step in a morphemic analysis is to segment the data, and this is done by comparing "pairs or sets of utterances which show partial contrast in both expression (sound) and content (grammatical meaning)." (Gleason 1961:66) MORPHEMIC ANALYSIS (MORPHOLOGY) is the process of identifying morphemes by means of comparing phonemically transcribed utterances which show contrast in *both* sound and meaning. "Two elements can be considered the same morpheme if 1) they have some common range of meaning, and 2) they are in complementary distribution conditioned by some phonological features." (Gleason 1961:80)

The task of morphemic analysis may be seen in the following example using data from the Zoque language spoken in Mexico.

Consider the following forms (from Nida 1949:21):

/ʔəs mpama/	*my clothes*	/pama/	*clothes*
/ʔəs ŋkayu/	*my horse*	/kayu/	*horse*
/ʔəs ntuwi/	*my dog*	/tuwi/	*dog*
/ʔəs mpoco/	*my younger sibling*	/poco/	*younger sibling*
/ʔəs ŋkose/	*my older sister*	/kose/	*older sister*
/ʔəs ncin/	*my pine*	/cin/	*pine*

From the data we can identify {ʔəs} as a morpheme which may be glossed as *my*. We also may identify six root morphemes on the basis of form and meaning uniqueness.

{pama}	*clothes*
{kayu}	*horse*
{tuwi}	*dog*
{poco}	*younger sibling*
{kose}	*older sister*
{cin}	*pine*

Note, however, that we have still not described the nasal prefixes. As Nida (1949:21) states:

The prefixal forms which occur in this series are m-, n-, and ŋ-. We say that they are assimilated to the following consonant, by which we mean that the alternant m- precedes the bilabial stop p, the alternant n- precedes the dental phonemes t and c, and the alternant ŋ- precedes the velar k.

The prefix is identified, despite its varied phonetic forms, as a single morpheme which may be glossed as POSSESSIVE PREFIX. The linguist chooses one form of the morpheme. For example, /n/ to represent the morpheme {n} and he lists it and other forms as allomorphs. Thus,

$$\{n\} \quad \text{possessive prefix}$$
$$\left.\begin{array}{c} /n/ \\ /m/ \\ /ŋ/ \end{array}\right\} \text{allomorphs}$$

Because it is possible to state which allomorph occurs given the initial consonant of the morpheme to which the prefix is attached, the allomorphs can be said to be in complementary distribution and phonologically conditioned:

$$/n/ \quad \text{occurs before dentals}$$
$$/m/ \quad \text{occurs before bilabials}$$
$$/ŋ/ \quad \text{occurs before velars}$$

On the basis of the known point and manner of articulation of these phonemes, data show that the dental allomorph of the nasal-prefix possessive morpheme occurs before dentals, the bilabial allomorph occurs before bilabials, and the velar allomorph before velars. This process is known as ASSIMILATION. In Chapter Two, we will see how such a relationship between pairs of sounds led to a new approach to describing languages based on such relationships. In the descriptive linguistic framework being discussed here, the sounds which occur together according to shared point of articulation are just listed and any relationship among such sets of sounds is left implicit.

Thus, in a formal description of this data, the results of the above morphemic analysis would be written:

{ʔəs}	*my*
{pama}	*clothes*
{tuwi}	*dog*
{poco}	*younger sibling*
{kose}	*older sister*
{cin}	*pine*
{n}	*possessive prefix*
	/n/ *occurs* /_____dentals
	/m/ *occurs* /_____bilabials
	/ŋ/ *occurs* /_____velars

The symbol (/), as opposed to (/ /) which encloses phonemic material, is read "in the environment of." Solid underlining, (_____) is a symbol which reads "before" or "after" and marks where the particular allomorph is placed. Thus, /n/ *occurs* /_____dentals*" reads that the /n/ allomorph of the morpheme {n} "possessive prefix" occurs where the possessive prefix is attached to a root beginning with a dental consonant.

Where we saw earlier that square brackets [ ] enclose phonetic material and slashes / / phonemes, the use of braces { } indicates "a morphemic representation in which one arbitrarily selected symbol is used to represent each morpheme and comprehend all its allomorphs. It does not directly give any information about pronunciation." (Gleason 1961:63)

Once all the morphemes have been identified in a body of speech data, the morphemes and allomorphs are arranged in STRUCTURAL CLASSES. For our purposes here, the morphemes identifiable in a body of data will be of a number of types, such as grammatical prefixes, roots, and possessive markers. When the morphemic analysis is written, the morphemes are arranged according to their distribution. This is done most generally with regard to which morphemes combine with which other morphemes or occur regularly with each other.

Such organization of morphemes into classes provides the basis for the next level of descriptive analysis known as SYNTAX. To the descriptive linguist, syntax is the description of the ways morphemes combine in utterances.

Before discussing this next higher level of the description of a body of speech data, it is necessary to touch briefly on a significant period in American descriptive linguistics. We have seen that Gleason's *An Introduction to Descriptive Linguis-*

tics (1961) codified the theory and method of descriptive linguistics. Between the time of Gleason's synthesis and Boas's and Sapir's earlier initiation of scientific linguistics, the field was greatly influenced by Leonard Bloomfield, particularly by his *Language* (1933).

In Bloomfield's view, the description of a body of speech data *is* a description of its phonemes and morphemes, beginning with a phonetic transcription. The concept of syntax as a level of description was only latent in his work and is a relatively late contribution to descriptive linguistic method and theory.

To Bloomfield, every complex form in a body of data is composed entirely of morphemes, and a complete list of the morphemes accounts for the phonetic forms in the data. In descriptive linguistics such a list is called a LEXICON and is composed of the morphemes identified and their glosses usually listed together. Bloomfield noted, though, that once the lexicon and phonemes of a body of speech data have been described, we might still fail to understand the forms of the language (1933:162). He observed that a speech description also must account for the order of succession of morphemes in utterances. This "meaningful arrangements of forms in language" he called grammar (1933:167).

The division between morphology and syntax became a controversial one. Since a main tenet of descriptive linguistics was that the student should thoroughly describe each level of a language before proceeding to the next higher level, deciding which forms are morphology and which are syntax became a crucial problem.

We saw above that morphemes are often *bound* forms (for example, attached to other morphemes such as prefixes and suffixes) as well as *free* forms (for example, independent "words"). To Bloomfield, grammar meant the meaningful arrangement of forms in the language. In this sense, grammar includes syntax as a statement of the order of occurrence of forms in a sentence and morphology as a list of the forms in the language which occur in sentences. In a Bloomfieldian description, grammar plus the lexicon, where the lexicon is a list of the morphemes in the language, constituted semantics. Thus, a descriptive linguistic analysis of a body of speech data of a particular language involved semantics and phonetics.

It is crucial here to make the point that, to Bloomfield, semantics (as grammar + lexicon) refers to meaning as form rather than content.

He believed that linguistics consists of the study of sounds (phonetics) and then the study of meaning (semantics). Semantics involved relating the sound features of language to its meaning features (Bloomfield, 1933:74). In his opinion, descriptive linguistics could not provide a way to link sound and meaning and still be "scientific": linguists were either mentalists or mechanists. A mechanist, Bloomfield presented a method in his book *Language* for a mechanistic analysis of spoken data. This analysis operated on the assumption that a scientist deals only with observable facts.

Defining meaning as the stimulus of the speaker in relation to the response of the hearer, Bloomfield, like Boas and Sapir, believed that it could and must be analyzed through form. Sapir hinted that there are degrees of abstractness in the ways that grammar (form) expresses concepts (meaning), but it was Bloomfield's rigorous method of linguistic analysis that determined the development of linguistics at that time as nonmentalist. Semantics, as the analysis of content, remains the least developed area of linguistic analysis.

Generally speaking, in the Bloomfield framework, morphology included the description of bound forms while syntactic constructions "are constructions in which none of the immediate constituents is a bound form." (1933:184)

IMMEDIATE CONSTITUENT ANALYSIS is *the* technique of syntactic analysis which dominated descriptive linguistics. A CONSTITUENT roughly is a form which occurs in conjunction with another form or forms but is not bound to it. For example, in the phrase *the old man, the* is a constituent of *old man.* Likewise *the* is a constituent of *old,* and *old* is a constituent of *man.*

From this, it is possible to see where problems arise as to the division between morphology and syntax. In English the division is haziest with compound words and certain phrase words. For example:

blackbird — compound word, as in *it's a blackbird not a robin*

jack-in-the-pulpit — phrase word as in *it's a jack-in-the-pulpit not a dahlia*

black bird—as in *it's a black bird not a red one*
Jack-in-the-pulpit—as in *it's Jack in the pulpit not Bill*

In a descriptive linguistic analysis of a body of data where phonetically transcribed data are formally analyzed and content may not be considered, the distinction between morphology and syntax is difficult to make on formal criteria alone. Based on the notion of bound forms versus constituents, it would be said that *blackbird* and *jack-in-the-pulpit* in (a) are morphemes while in (b) *black* and *bird* are constituents of each other and *Jack, in, the, pulpit* are constituents of each other and the construction is syntactic.

Thus, morphology is the analysis of the minimal units of language which have a formal meaning. The morphology of a language is a description of the "constructions in which bound forms appear among the constituents. By definition, the resultant forms are either bound forms or words but never phrases. Accordingly, we may say that morphology includes the construction of words and parts of words, while syntax includes the construction of phrases." (1933:207)

We will see in the following section that a number of proposals for syntactic description have been advanced and have had a great influence on descriptive linguistics and linguistics in general.

Syntax

The next level of analysis within a descriptive framework is that of syntactic analysis.

> Syntax may be roughly defined as the principles of arrangement of the constructions formed by the process of derivation and inflection (words) into larger constructions of various kinds. (Gleason 1961:128)

The method of analysis at the syntactic level involves searching for immediate constituents within utterances by comparing samples. For example, given the utterance "Those three sophomores ate my pepperoni pizza," an immediate constituent analysis (henceforth, IC analysis), segmenting the sentence into its constituents, would yield cuts in the following way:

Those three sophomores/ ate my pepperoni pizza.
Those three sophomores/ ate/ my pepperoni pizza.
Those/ three sophomores/ ate/ my/ pepperoni pizza.
Those/ three/ sophomores/ ate/ my/ pepperoni/ pizza.

The sentence is broken up into its major constituents, amounting here first to the total subject and the total predicate. The next cut separates the constituents of the subject and of the predicate respectively and so forth until all constituents of the utterance have been marked. There are two ways of analyzing an utterance. One is by identifying its immediate constituents, working from the utterance to the morpheme as in this example. The other is by moving from the morpheme to the utterance. In proceeding from morpheme to utterance, constituent cuts are progressively erased, forming larger and larger constituents back to the utterance itself. In other words, one moves from step 4 to step 1. This was the original method proposed and parallels procedures of phonemic and morphemic analysis. That is, IC analysis of an utterance beginning at the level of morphemes would begin by combining morphemes into phrases and then phrases into sentences or utterances. For example:

    {*ate*} (actually {*eat*} + {past})
    {*three*} + {sophomores} (actually {*sophomore*} + {plural})
    {*pepperoni*}+ {*pizza*}
    {*those*} + {*three*} + {*sophomores*}
    {*my*}+ {*pepperoni*} + {*pizza*}
    {*ate*} + {*my*} + {*pepperoni*} + {*pizza*}
    {*those*} + {*three*} + {*sophomores*} + {*ate*} + {*my*} +
    {*pepperoni*} + {*pizza*}

Such an approach is called COMBINATORY. The end result after combining the morphemes progressively as they "go together" is a distinct unit, an utterance, or a sentence. This process is similar to what was done in phonemics, combining allophones into distinct units — phonemes, and in morphemics, combining allomorphs into distinct units — morphemes.

By way of review, then, descriptive linguistics as presented by Gleason has the following steps:

Phonology (Phonetic and Phonemics)
1. Gather body of data and transcribe it phonetically
2. Phonemic analysis
   list phonemes and allophones
Grammar (Morphology or Word Grammar and Syntax or Sentence Grammar)
3. Morphemic analysis
   list morphemes and allomorphs in structural classes
4. Syntactic analysis
   mark off immediate constituents of an utterance.

The morpheme-to-utterance procedure of IC analysis was largely developed by the American linguist Zellig Harris. It is useful to think of IC analysis "as an attempt to make more rigorous the traditional notion of parsing" sentences. (Chomsky 1958:124)

Although IC analysis was developed as the next higher level of description of a body of speech data after morphemics and was intended to involve a set of discovery procedures (as did phonemics and morphemics), the results of the analysis seemed to lack the rigor of the descriptions at lower levels. Nonetheless *the* model of syntactic description which is generally tied to the methods used by linguists to describe languages in their own terms is this IC analysis model.

We will see how proposals to formalize IC analysis going from utterance to morpheme rather than morpheme to utterance provided an impetus to the development of what is known as transformational/generative grammar. Since phonemics, morphemics, and immediate constituent analysis as procedures for describing a body of speech data usually proceeded from the "bottom to the top" or from the smallest units of analysis to the more complex, not surprisingly the idea of proceeding from the larger complex unit to a formal analysis of its components was considered revolutionary. This innovative approach to linguistic analysis radically changed the target of linguistic analysis. Eventually, some linguists abandoned the notion of levels of language per se as being hierarchically ordered.

To begin an analysis of a language by attempting to describe the structure of whole utterances would entail a set of assumptions substantially different from those of the descriptive linguist. One such new assumption was that the linguist could no longer mechanically refine a body of speech data (as utterances) without some prior knowledge of the language (as structure and meaning).

Part of the impetus for the new ideas for describing language structure as well as speech data may be seen in certain problems which arose in attempting to carry out IC analysis. Consider the following sentences:

> *The pizza was eaten by sophomores.*
> *The pizza was eaten by morning.*

An IC analysis of these sentences would produce the same results for each. For example:

$$The/\ pizza/\ was/\ eaten/\ by/ \begin{cases} sophomores \\ morning \end{cases}$$

$$The\ pizza/\ was/\ eaten/ \begin{matrix} by\ sophomores \\ by\ morning \end{matrix}$$

$$The\ pizza/\ was\ eaten/ \begin{matrix} by\ sophomores \\ by\ morning \end{matrix}$$

$$The\ pizza/ \begin{matrix} was\ eaten\ by\ sophomores \\ was\ eaten\ by\ morning \end{matrix}$$

The pizza was eaten by sophomores
The pizza was eaten by morning

The method of IC analysis provides no way to distinguish *by* of the passive (*by the sophomores* as agent) and *by* as a preposition *by the morning* as an adverb phrase). (cf. Harris 1954:162)

In a morphemic analysis preceding the IC analysis of a body of data containing sentences such as these, the *two* morphemes {by} would have been identified and listed: one as "agent" and the other as a "preposition" and glossed as such. However, in combining morphemes progressively into utterances using the technique of IC analysis, the distinction made at the morphemic level is lost. Where it was clear at the morphemic level that there are two morphemes {by}, at the syntactic level it appears that in terms of how {by} combines in constituents that there is no difference. IC analysis provides no procedural way for the linguist to describe the difference between the two sentences. In fact, a descriptive linguist would likely assume that the two utterances have the same structural description, while any native speaker would "know" that the sentences are quite different. Further, a native speaker "knows" that the sentences differ at a level not explicable by the lexical difference between *sophomores* and *morning*.

The basic idea of IC analysis, that it is possible to describe the utterances of a language "in terms of the co-occurrence of individual morphemes," was called into question. (Harris 1957:285) The example above (*The pizza was eaten by sophomores* vs. *The pizza was eaten by morning*) in light of one other sentence plus an unacceptable sentence, such as *The sophomores ate pizza* or *The morning ate cheese*, demonstrates that analysis based on the occurrence of morphemes in the same slot in an utterance obscures some facts of the language. Harris's work beyond IC analysis has been said to have "brought to light a serious inadequacy of modern linguistic theory, namely, its inability to account for such systematic relations between sentences as the active-passive relation." (Chomsky 1958:124)

If we recall the idea in descriptive linguistics that meaning was held not to be the concern of the linguist and, as well, out of grasp, then this failure to analyze sentences such as *The pizza was eaten by sophomores* and *The pizza was eaten by morning* as different does not appear to be as significant. Yet it is clear to a native speaker of English that an analysis of these two sentences as having the same constituent structure may describe the facts yet leave "something" still unanalyzed grammatically. This "something" will be seen in Chapter Two to be the structure of the language (*langue*) as differentiated from its manifestation in a body of speech data (*parole*).

It must be emphasized here that IC analysis was and is a technique for mechanically combining morphemes into the progressively larger units (constituents) of an utterance and it provides a way for describing the observed facts of a body of data.

An article by Rulon Wells titled "Immediate Constituents" (1957) is considered the classical statement of the immediate constituent approach in American linguistics. Wells saw IC analysis to be the hierarchical bracketing of a string of morphemes into usually continuous segments. But, the classical formulation signaled a break with traditional descriptive linguistics, suggesting that analysis always operate procedurally from utterance (a string) to morphemes (its segments), that is, from the top down. This formulation set the stage for representing the structure of sentences on labeled tree diagrams. It figured significantly in the development of what became known as PHRASE-STRUCTURE GRAMMAR.

An example of Wells's IC analysis would be

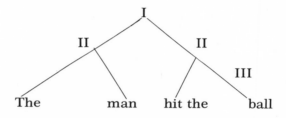

In Chapter Two we will see this same sentence analyzed in a phrase structure grammar approach.

Descriptive linguistics is still the basic and the most useful approach for describing speech data if the linguist is unfamiliar with the language being spoken. Phonemics and morphemics are accepted procedures for describing the minimal units of sound and grammatical or formal meaning in the speech of informants. Where description of speech data is the linguist's goal, descriptive linguistics offers the most rigorous way of accurately presenting the observed facts.

As Noam Chomsky (1958:212) notes regarding the task and procedure of descriptive linguistics:

> The central methodological concern in recent American linguistics has been the precise definition of such notions as PHONEME, MORPHEME, and IMMEDIATE CONSTITUENT. Almost without exception, phonemes have been thought of in relatively substantial terms as . . . certain classes of sounds, while

morphemes are taken to be certain classes of sequences of phonemes. The methodological problem for linguistic theory, then, has been to provide the general criteria for making these classifications, and the goal of the linguistic analysis of a particular language has been to isolate and list the particular classes, sequences, sequences of classes, etc., which are the phonemes, morphemes, constituents of these languages. A linguistic grammar of a particular language, in this view, is an inventory of elements, and linguistics is thought of as a classificatory science.

Ironically, Chomsky has been and remains critical of descriptive linguistics. His criticism focuses not on the validity of the field's techniques for classifying the data but on the notion of describing speech as a means of studying language scientifically. His goals and those of the field-working descriptivist differ on the following grounds:

> Neither the conception of a grammar as an inventory of elements nor the requirement that there be a discovery procedure for elements of the inventory is very easy to justify. A grammar of a language should at least be expected to offer a characterization of the set of objects that are sentences of this language, i.e, to enable its user to construct a list or enumeration of these utterances. It is not at all clear how an inventory of elements provides this information . . . . (1958:212)

Moreover, descriptivists saw the focus of linguistics as being methodological and its task being that of elaborating "techniques for discovering and classifying linguistic elements." (Chomsky 1958:24) Once the elements were discovered and classified, a grammar, defined as inventories of linguistic elements and classes, could be produced.

Structural linguists and transformational grammarians define a grammar differently. The former use the notion of the system and apply it to language in general; the latter define a grammar as a theory of language. The descriptivists seek to describe collectable linguistic data. Structuralists and transformationalists aim to describe abstract linguistic systems of relational elements that underlie speech. IC analysis, in addition to presenting a methodological problem to the descriptive linguist, influenced the development of structural linguistics. Language began to be looked at as an abstract structure *(langue)* as well as the set of samples of collected speech *(parole)*. Linguistics as a science had become more than the developing of procedures for describing speech.

Summary

For the first half of the twentieth century, linguistics was defined as a scientific endeavor engaged in developing precise and rigorous methods of analysis. Descriptive linguistics – the basic branch of linguistic science during those decades – consisted of phonology dealing with phonemes and grammar dealing with morphemes and their combinations. As for linguistics as a science defined this way, Gleason (1961:11) could say that in some respects it had "developed more precise and rigorous methods and attained more definitive results than any other science dealing with human behavior."

Provided with the phoneme and morpheme as basic units, linguists could use them "to build a comprehensive theory of the expression side of language" (speech) and to make statements as to what illustrates speech (expression). To descriptive linguists, speech had a structure of sounds (phonemes) and grammatical units composed of sound sequences (morphemes). Different languages employ differently structured speech yet the structural differences are describable in terms of the different sets of phonemes the languages have and in terms of the different morphemes and morpheme combinations that speakers employ. The statement of the phonemic and grammatical systems of the world's languages constitutes for the descriptive linguist an analysis of the internal structure of the expression or speech aspect of language. After all, a language's speech structure "is the sum of the patterns of arrangement" of phonemes and morphemes in that language (Gleason 1961: 11). To the descriptivist "linguistics is the science which attempts to understand language from the point of view of its internal structure." (Gleason 1961:2) Work on describing the speech structure of a language has not developed successfully.

Descriptive linguists see the need to attend to the analysis of the content as well as the expression of speech. Furthermore, they know the difficulties encountered in gaining access to the structure of content. Delimiting content is more difficult than delimiting expression. While expression is constrained by the physiology of speech, content in substance appears to involve "the whole of human experience." (Gleason 1961:13) In part, content as intruding on the description of expression was a factor in the problems encountered in the analysis of syntax using immediate constituents. Deciding where to make IC cuts involved inferences which could not rest on mechanical procedures of observing the data. As Gleason (1961:149) noted: "To understand the sentence, the hearer must deduce the IC structure, or something having many of the same properties. Otherwise the meaning will elude him."

The need for deducing meaning and analyzing at least some of the structure of the content of speech in order to describe speech as expression led some linguists to decide that the science of linguistics might profit from shifting its focus away from speech altogether. This shift changed linguistics from the unified descriptive science of the early twentieth century into a science of language with two objectives. Descriptivists continued to analyze speech as well as work on ways to describe the internal structure of content. A new branch of linguistics called structuralist focused on the internal structure of language as a system of relationships rather than on the internal structure of the expression, content, and vocabulary aspects of speech. The structuralists are our concern in the next chapter.

For thought and discussion

1. What does it mean to understand the "phenomenon of language"? Describe the techniques developed by descriptive linguistics to achieve this goal. Why might descriptions of languages *not* be sufficient to understand languages? What does it mean to say that language is more than speech?

2. What does it mean to study language as opposed to studying a language? How are the methods devised for studying individual languages useful in studying language in general?

3. If we regard language primarily as sound, what distinguishes language from other types of sound such as alarms? What about sound systems such as the Morse Code—is this language?

4. Boas believed that three points had to be considered in an objective discussion of languages: the constituent phonetic elements of the language, the clusters of ideas expressed by phonetic groups, and the methods of combining and modifying phonetic groups. What ideas are expressed by phonetic groups?

5. Why should the flap R sound occurring in some dialects when /d/ and /t/ are found between vowels (ladder and latter) be considered an allophone of both /t/ and /d/? Why is the sound [ɚ] when it occurs in *the* [əi] not considered an allophone of the sound [ə] in *with*? Why is it important to distinguish between phonetic elements and phonemes?

6. Why is the rule that realizes the plural morpheme in English as either /z/, /s/, or /əz/ phonologically conditioned? Is there a similar rule for the *ed* suffix of the past tense in English? Is it also phonologically conditioned? How would a linguist describing English determine that the *ren* and *es* in child*ren* and hors*es* have a common range of meaning?

7. Can something be an allomorph without being an allophone? Why? Give examples.

8. What happens to /f/ in the plural forms of self, wife, and half? What is the environment for change? Can a generalization be made?

9. Why is a lexicon not enough to describe a language? What is the problem you encounter, for instance, when trying to communicate in a foreign language with only a dictionary at your disposal? How does this relate to what Bloomfield says about the study of language?

10. What is meant by the statement "In linguistics the only type of meaning which can be studied is that expressed by form?" Do you agree? Why does this analysis not account for sentences such as *The boy may frighten sincerity* and *The boy is abundant*?

11. If we compare the study of syntax to the study of phonemes

and morphemes, then how would you describe a hypothetical SYNTACTEME, the smallest meaningful unit of the syntax? Give an example. Explain your reasoning. Would there be any formal relation between the sentences *Sophomores ate the pizza* and *The pizza was eaten by sophomores*? Would this take care of the problem of the phrases *by morning* and *by sophomores*? (see p. 28).

12. Using the terms LANGUAGE DESCRIPTION and LINGUISTIC THEORY as defined on page 2, how do you think each would differ in its analysis of English? (See quotes on pp. 30 and 31.)

TWO

Structural Linguistics

Development and Goals of Structural Linguistics

Structural linguistics attempts to study the unconscious structure of language. It is concerned with the relations between the units as the important data rather than the units themselves, operating on the assumption that the underlying structure of language is systemic, with the goal of discovering general laws of language. Structural linguistic data are relations between terms (items, units, elements, things) rather than the terms themselves. Descriptive linguistics analysis, in contrast, is concerned with isolating the terms at various levels of description from within a body of speech data.[1] The descriptive method emphasizes the isolation of elements such as phonemes and morphemes. Therefore, mixing descriptive levels within that framework is taboo. A language's sound system must be described in terms of the distinctive units employed within it. Morphemes, the minimal yet meaningful units of sound, are at a "higher" level of description. Although morphemes are made up of phonemes (and only those phonemes distinctive for the language being described), they are described as minimal distinctive units separately and at a morphemic level of description. Each level of a linguistic description must be kept separate and described that way.

As an illustration, consider the contrast between the phonemes /t/ and /d/ in English. Some English speakers pronounce *latter* and *ladder* the same way. The descriptive linguist who is working on English, but does not know the language and is unable to use information at "higher" or "different" levels of description, is hindered in deciding which of the phonemes, /t/ or /d/, is in each word.

Gleason (1961:294–295) considered this example and presented a solution which most American linguists would choose. He suggested that the language be analyzed as having "a system of six stops in some positions [phonetic environments] only five in others." For example:

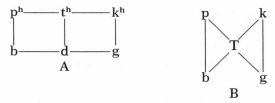

Figure 2 – 1. English Stop Consonants

The descriptive linguist's task of matching up these systems involves equating the [T] (Figure 2-1B) in the positions where five stops occur with each of the two alveolar stops, [tʰ] or [d], (Figure 2-1A) occurring in positions where six occur. The descriptive linguist must decide whether *latter* and *ladder*, when they both sound the same, are both /lǽdər/ or both /lǽtər/ and whether one, *ladder*, is always /lǽdər/ and *latter* is optionally /lǽtər/ and /lǽdər/ in the same speaker.

As Gleason (1961:275) explains

> If the match is to be made, there must be an appeal to phonetics and a careful study of the ranges of variation of the stops under discussion. In some such instances the phonetic charac-

teristics of the sounds involved will render the decision quite obvious. In other instances it may be a very delicate decision. In occasional instances the decision can only be made arbitrarily. Of course, the *difficult decisions will also have to be faced, in a different guise perhaps, in any other approach* (Emphasis mine).

In contrast to this solution of the problem, Gleason also mentions a different solution "some Europeans" would use: the theory and method of structural linguistics. In so doing, he spotlights the differences between the descriptivist and the structuralist schools of linguistics. Essentially the European solution would permit units such as /T/ in which the voiced/voiceless contrast is lost or, in structuralist words, neutralized. The structuralist need not know which phoneme occurs medially in *latter* and *ladder* as long as the sound occurring interrelates with the sound system of the language under study.

Gleason's diagram of the six stops occurring in some positions versus the five occurring in other positions may also be seen as a diagram showing a series of six English stop sounds related to each other in the sound system of English in the same way. In other words,

$$[p^h] \text{ is to } [b] \text{ as } [t^h] \text{ is to } [d] \text{ as } [k^h] \text{ is to } [g].$$

The relationship may be seen as one of the voiceless /p/, /t/, /k/ versus the voiced /b/, /d/, /g/. For the stop occurring between the vowels, English speakers who do not distinguish *latter* from *ladder* use a sound having the features of [t^h] and [d], except that in this intervocalic environment it does not matter whether the sound is voiced like [d] or voiceless and aspirated like [t^h]. The structural linguist is interested in the fact that [p^h] and [b], [t^h] and [d], and [k^h] and [g] are all terms related to each other in a VOICED/VOICELESS OPPOSITION. In describing such a relationship among terms or sounds, the structuralist focuses on those features of opposition and similarity rather than on demonstrating that a /t/ is always a /t/ or a /d/ always a /d/.

Within the structuralist framework, the voicing distinction between /t/ and /d/ for some speakers of English would be neutralized when they occur between vowels. Moreover, a structuralist analysis of the sound system of English would show that *latter* and *ladder* are pronounced [lǽtər] and/or [lǽdər] may be analyzed as [lǽTər].

Actually, the structuralists are much more interested in the relationships among sound features such as voicing than in isolating the sounds as separate units with associated sound features. Their position is that we know more about English by being able to say that the phonemic elements [pʰ] and [b] are related to each other in the same way that [tʰ] and [d] are than we do by showing that English has a /p/ and a /b/ and a /t/ and a /d/ and that minimal pairs can be found showing these sounds as distinctive in various positions in a word.

Much of structural linguistics today has also been incorporated into descriptive linguistics. Gleason's example in his *Descriptive Linguistics* (2nd ed., 1961) shows that descriptivists were considering some of the techniques and ideas of structuralism from Europe.

The more recent type of descriptive linguistics as described by Gleason (1961) and by Harris (1951) which incorporates some structuralist notions is often called American structural linguistics. This approach aims at language description and preserves the idea that methods and discovery procedures are imperative in describing data. From this same base a new linguistic emphasis emerged, moving from working only with objectively verifiable data toward an analysis of language as an abstract system with universal properties and relationships.

Linguists today who work with data they gathered on a language which they do not speak natively and who employ descriptive and American structuralist techniques are often called ANTHROPOLOGICAL LINGUISTS.

Structuralism, a highly popular, theoretical approach to the broader study of culture (including language), is directly related to the structural linguistics which began as the "European solution" Gleason ascribes to descriptive problems. Prior to the "European solution," linguistics was essentially the description of transcribed speech even in its efforts to deal with comparative and historical issues.

We will now focus on the main elements of structural linguistics which fostered the division of the science of language into current linguistic theory (abstract and theoretical) and language description (objective and applied).

Distinctive Features and the Emergence of the Systematic Phoneme

Remember that there were two ways of assigning phonemic status to the medial consonant. Descriptive linguists would try to match the sound with others in the same environment in the language (such as the sound in *tattle* [tætəl] or *paddle* [pædəl]) and decide where the segmental entity occurred medially in the word. Structural linguists, however, would note that the sounds are not distinguished with respect to the feature of voicing and thus focus on a relationship which often holds among regularly distinct sounds in the system.

N. S. Trubetzkoy, a Russian prince and noted member of the "Prague School of Linguistics," is primarily credited with formulating the "European solution." He noted that "phonological contrasts which are suspended in certain positions [suspendible or neutralizable contrasts] take on a specific character in those positions in which they cannot be suspended." (1935:27)

The ideas of Trubetzkoy and others emerged and took form at an international linguistics conference held in Prague, Czechoslovakia, in the early 1930s. The ideas entered America largely through the work of Roman Jakobson who used theories of Prague School linguists "to dissolve language into its ultimate components, the dyadic distinctive features." (1956: preface)

Before examining the idea of distinctive features in phonology as presented by Jakobson along with Morris Halle (1956), we must first review the state of linguistic science in Europe in the 1930s and '40s and compare it with the American situation as discussed in Chapter One. Doing so will enable us to see the framework upon which these notions of systematic features and values were built.

Largely because of the influence of Émile Durkheim, the French sociologist and philosopher, European scholars early in this century shifted their concerns from individual behavior to group behavior. Ferdinand deSaussure, a Swiss linguist, applied Durkheim's idea of the importance of collective consciousness to structural linguistics. He divided linguistics into *la parole* (individual speech acts), *la langage* (individual

speech acts + rules of language), and *la langue* (rules of language).
In his view:

> *La langue* is the set of passively acquired habits we have been taught by our speech community, in terms of which we understand other speakers and produce combinations other speakers of our community understand. When we hear *la parole* of another community we perceive the noises made, but not the social fact of language. We cannot connect the sounds produced and the social facts, according to a set of rules. These rules, which can be called the convention, or grammar of the language are habits that education has imposed upon us. (Dinneen 1967:197)

This view can be explained by comparing *la langue* to Durkheim's collective consciousness.

> . . . *la langue* is the social fact, being general throughout a community and exercising constraint over the individual speakers. . . [it] is not found complete and perfect in any individual. *La parole* includes anything a speaker might say; *la langue* encompasses anything a speaker might say well as the constraints that prevent him from saying anything ungrammatical. *(Ibid.)*

To deSaussure, linguistics ought to deal *only* with the study of *la langue* and the study of *la langue* ought to consider the common patterns shared by all speakers.

Linguistics was viewed solely as the study of *la langue*, and upon this consensus the idea of phonological distinctive features developed. DeSaussure held that *la langue* is a stable set of relations among linguistic entities. Hardly surprising, phonologists interested in the shared sounds in a speech community then turned toward seeking the relationships between sound entities as linguistic signs.

DeSaussure introduced two more ideas that later influenced the development of distinctive feature phonology: PARADIGMATIC and SYNTAGMATIC RELATIONS. Linguistic entities occurring in linear sequence are SYNTAGMS. A syntagmatic relationship exists in the opposition a syntagm has to everything before and after it. For example, in *bit* /bIt/, /b/ stands in a syntagmatic relation to /I/ and /I/ to /b/. Moreover, /I/ has a syntagmatic relation to /t/ and vice versa.

ASSOCIATIVE RELATIONS, now more commonly known as paradigmatic relations, occur at a more abstract and simultaneous plane. For example, in /bIt/, the /b/ is in a paradigmatic relationship with a /p/ since many of the features of both sounds occur simultaneously. Conceivably, a listener might ask, "Did you say *bit* or *pit*?" — not "Did you say *bit* or *sag*?"

According to deSaussure (1916:123), the syntagmatic relation may be regarded as overt, surface, or autonomous and the paradigmatic as covert, deep, or systematic.

Having reviewed the notions of *la langue, la parole, la langage,* syntagm, and paradigm, we may now discuss the development of phonological distinctive features and more clearly understand the segmental phonemic analysis/systematic structural phonetic bifurcation which developed in linguistics. We will see that attention shifted from isolating linguistic entities which occur linearly in *la parole* to stating associative relations occurring among linguistic entities simultaneously in *la langue.* Distinctive feature phonology is the study of the simultaneously occurring features of sound which interrelate in *la langue.*

In fact, distinctive features, the minimal entities which differentiate sounds, stand in a paradigmatic relation to each other in the minds of speech specialists. For example, Bloomfield borrowed, or possibly "coined," the term *distinctive feature* and applied it to phonemes as real and observable entities. To him, distinctive features occurred in phonemes.

Interestingly, the descriptive linguists seemed bent on isolating phonemes. The structuralists were interested in what constituted phonemes. Whereas Bloomfield wanted to identify the entities of *la parole* which entered into syntagmatic relations with each other, Jakobson and other linguists wanted to find the entities of *la langue* which opposed each other paradigmatically.

In 1956, Jakobson and Halle incorporated the ideas of the Prague linguists and of deSaussure for the study of sound in *la langue.* Trying to explain how language uses sound matter, they called the discipline concerned with this question (systematic) phonology, thereby relegating the term (autonomous or taxonomic) phonemics to what they considered to be a separate field. This was an early distinction made between linguistic theory and language description.

Jakobson and Halle claimed that a set of INHERENT DISTINCTIVE FEATURES in the world's languages which, in addition to qualities such as pitch, loudness, and duration, "underlie their entire lexical and morphological stock [and] amount to twelve oppositions, out of which each language makes its own selection." (1956:29)

Each feature has an acoustic and an articulatory definition. The sound spectrograph makes it possible to view the formants on a voice print made by sounds as heard. A sound spectrograph displays the energy produced at different sound frequencies on a graph. The graph or voice print is a spectrum which shows a sound's frequency and intensity.

This dual nature of a distinctive feature reflects the emphasis on viewing sounds and the sound rules of a speech community in terms of both the speaker (the articulatory aspect) and the hearer (the acoustic aspect). Conversely, as was the case with phonemics, sounds were described in the descriptive linguistic framework as separate entities in articulatory terms alone. It was necessary only to describe where and how the speaker made the sound.

Jakobson and Halle (1956:29–32) found that twelve oppositions occur in the world's languages:

1. vocalic/nonvocalic
    +vocalic = a sharp structure (called a formant) appears on the sound spectrograph recording and air passes unobstructed from the glottis through the vocal tract.
2. consonantal/nonconsonantal
    +consonantal = low total energy is shown on the spectrograph, and such a sound involves air being obstructed in the vocal tract.
3. compact/diffuse
    +compact = initially high energy is shown in a narrow central region of the spectrographic recording followed by an increase in the total amount of

energy shown. A compact sound is "forward flanged" — in other words, the volume of the resonance chamber is greater in front of the place of narrowest stricture of the vocal tract (for example, /k/ and /g/ are +compact).

4. tense/lax

+tense = high energy is shown on the spectrograph plus a great spread of energy on the recording in space and time. Tense sounds involve a great degree of involvement of the vocal tract "away from its rest position" (for example, /i/ is tense versus /I/ which is lax).

5. voiced/voiceless

+voice = the spectrograph shows periodic movement of low frequency. A voiced sound is made by periodic vibrations of the vocal cords (for example, /d/ versus /t/).

6. nasal/oral

+nasal = energy is spread over a wider range of frequency on the graph of the print by reducing the intensity of the first formants and introducing added (nasal) formants. Nasal sounds involve supplementing the use of the oral cavity with the nasal cavity (for example, /n/ is +nasal versus /d/ which is —nasal).

7. discontinuous/continuant

+discontinuous = an abrupt transition appears between such a sound and silence. A discontinuous sound involves a "rapid turning on or off" of the energy source by rapidly opening or closing the vocal tract. A flap or trill /r/ is discontinuous in contrast or opposition to an /l/.

8. strident/mellow

+strident = "high intensity noise." A strident sound is "rough-edged." Such sounds have supplementary obstruction at the point of articulation in the mouth. For example, /θ/ and /ð/ are strident sounds.

9. checked/unchecked

+checked = a high rate of energy is discharged in a short

period of time. The glottal stop /ʔ/ and glottalized
sounds are +checked.

10. grave/acute

+grave = the energy is shown on the spectrum to be
concentrated in the lower frequencies. Articulatorily, grave sounds are made at the periphery of
the mouth (for example, /p/ and /b/ and /k/ and
/g/) while acute sounds are made in the middle of
the mouth and have a more "compartmental-
ized" resonator.

11. flat/plain

+flat = a sound where some upper frequency formants
show a downward shift. Flat sounds in an artic-
ulatory-only description were called narrow-slit
sounds. In other words, the vocal tract or mouth
resonator orifice size is decreased or constricted
either in front or back; /w/ is a +flat sound, as are
sounds which are said to be velarized.

12. sharp/plain

+sharp = some upper frequency components of such
sounds show an upward shift. Acoustically,
+sharp sounds are referred to as "wide-slit" and
show a "dilated pharyngeal pass." In other words,
the back orifice of the mouth resonator is evident
and palatalization occurs to restrict the cavity of
the mouth; /č/ and /ǰ/ are +sharp sounds.

The twelve oppositions are what is important here. The reader is not expected to be able to interpret a spectrogram based on
these definitions. The opposition features are defined in order
to indicate that both sound production (articulation) and recep-
tion (acoustics) are considered in a structuralist phonological
analysis. Gleason's chapter on acoustic phonetics (1961:
357–372) provides a readable account of how to interpret spec-
trographic representations of articulated sounds so that one
may see more clearly how these features seek to match acoustic and articulatory definitions of sound.

Since 1956, feature names and definitions have undergone
substantial revision. Chomsky and Halle's *The Sound Pattern
of English* (1968), for example, expands the theory behind the

features as well as their definitions in the specialty of modern linguistics known as GENERATIVE PHONOLOGY. The twelve features posited by Jakobson and Halle form the basis of the structuralist phonology and as such serve along with their theoretical underpinnings as the foundations of the new field of generative phonology. Using the twelve pairs of features and recognizing the systemic and interrelated nature of phonology in language, the conventional view of investigating sound changed between 1930 and 1960 from a *taxonomic* or *autonomous phonemics* to a view known as *systematic phonology*. By the early 1960s systematic phonology had gained wide currency in America and began evolving beyond an interest in the oppositions themselves (the specific features such as vocalic/nonvocalic, grave/acute, compact/diffuse) to an interest in devising sets of rules which show the process whereby phonetic material is realized variously as the phonological structure of language.

> The phonetic representation of an utterance consists of a string of *phonetic segments* each of which is a complex of independent multivalue features describing some aspect of the ideal behavior of the speech apparatus . . . the phonological representation of an utterance consists exhaustively of a string of symbols of some kind . . . the task of the phonological rules is to map phonological strings into phonetic ones. (Postal 1968:53)

Systematic phonology may be seen as a moderate position compared to autonomous (or taxonomic or descriptive) phonemics in that, in the systematic view, phonetic structure provides "a substantial, but far from complete, portion of the information relevant for the determination of phonological structure, the rest being provided by grammatical information, i.e., information about word boundaries, morpheme boundaries, syntactic and morphological categorizations, morphophonemic alternations, etc." (Postal 1958:56, fn. 3)

As stressed in Chapter One, in addition to the goals and purposes of descriptive linguistics, such looking at other levels of description was both taboo and, given the constraints of the linguist (never having prior contact with the language being described), impossible.

In the next section, we will discuss the American structuralist notion of *long components* as this idea figured in separating the emerging dichotomous groups of linguists into those for abstract representation of language versus those interested in adequate descriptions of languages.

The origins of systematic phonology in the Prague School and the work of Jakobson and Halle signal a shift from the work initiated by Boas and Sapir which did not use the notion of sound features but rather focused on phonemes as entities discoverable in linearly transcribed phonetic data.

Long Components

European structuralist views particularly influenced Zellig Harris, the American linguist. In a paper, "Simultaneous Components in Phonology" (1944), he set out to compare the merits of describing language in terms of paradigmatic (simultaneous features) relations of items versus syntagmatic (linear sound segment) occurrences of items. He also questioned the usefulness of a paradigmatic approach for descriptive linguistics.

> At present [i.e., in American descriptive linguistics] the phonemic elements of linguistic analysis are obtained by segmenting the flow of speech and calling each group of mutually substitutable segments ("free variants") an allophone. Now the components described in this paper are not complete physical events; therefore, they cannot actually be substituted for each other to see if any two of them are free variants or "repetitions" of each other. (1944 as in Joos, ed., 1963:136)

Thus, Harris observed that as long as the task is to discover and isolate segmental entities in speech, the component or feature approach would hinder the task and, for many purposes, phonemes remain in his view the most convenient representations of speech. (1951:125, note 2)

Nonetheless, Harris developed a procedure for analyzing taxonomic or autonomous phonemes into what he called LONG COMPONENTS "so as to yield new phonologic elements, fewer in number and less restricted in distribution." (1951:125, note 2)

An example of a long component and the procedure whereby it is analyzed would be to observe that the consonant cluster /sp/ occurs in the speech of some English speakers as in *inspire* but those speakers may have no /sb/ cluster in their speech, while they do have a /zb/ as in *asbestos, husband,* and *rasperry.* From these observations, according to Harris, we may define

$$/sp/ = /\overline{zb}/ \quad \text{In other words, /sp/ is to } /\overline{zb}/ \text{ as}$$
$$/s/ \ = /\overline{z}/ \qquad\qquad /s/ \ \text{ is to } /\overline{z}/ \text{ as}$$
$$/p/ \ = /\overline{b}/ \qquad\qquad /p/ \ \text{ is to } /\overline{b}/.$$

The long component (noted by the bar extending over it) is defined as the difference between voiceless and voiced. (Harris 1951:128) By discovering long components it is possible to make generalizations regarding the occurrence of segments in sequence. That is, it is possible to state, for a language which has the above-defined long component, that where a bilabial stop (p,b) and an alveolar fricative (spirant, s, z) co-occur, the two as a cluster will both either be voiced or voiceless.

To the descriptive linguist, this is a help if we remember that the task there is to decide, when an utterance is transcribed such as [spIn] in English, whether the [p] is an allophone of /p/ or of /b/.

The extracting of components or features which have an effect over segments co-occurring will facilitate such a decision. If the initial sound is a voiceless spirant[s], the following stop is also voiceless. Therefore, [p] in [spIn] is an allophone of /p/ and */sbIn/ does not conform to the sound pattern of English.[2]

Harris's notion of long components was an attempt to lend more sophistication to taxonomic segmental phonemic analysis by trying to broaden it to include phonemic segments in linear sequence. His view on applying structuralist ideas was that, to American descriptive linguistics,

> The phonemes were set up so as to be the least restricted successive . . . elements representing speech. Therefore, the only possiblilities for further analysis lie in the direction of changing our segments. The chief opportunity which we can now find for changing our elements is to consider each segment as susceptible of analysis into simultaneously occurring component elements. (1951:125)

The interesting aspect of Harris's focus on simultaneously occurring features is in his view of their actual co-occurrence in linear sequences of speech. In order to describe the sound features in context, Harris found himself in a position of advocating the use of knowledge gleaned from other descriptive levels.

This need to appeal to other levels of description led to the development of the MORPHOPHONEME, a term used by a number of earlier linguists including Sapir and Trubetzkoy. Harris observed that once long components affecting the representation of sounds in sequence can be extracted, it is also possible to observe in a body of speech data that not only do some morphemes have different allomorphs, but that often the allomorphs may be determined by phonological conditions because of constraints on the sequential occurrence of sounds in the language. Consequently, not only may one account for *spin* as an acceptable English word as opposed to **sbin*,[2] but also it is possible to find relationships as long components which allow the linguist to account for [waif] *wife* (singular) but [waivz] *wives* (plural) versus [waifs] *wife's* possessive. Therefore, we define:

$$/\text{fs}/ = /\overline{\text{vz}}/$$
$$/\text{f}/ \ \ = /\bar{\text{v}}/$$
$$/\text{s}/ \ \ = /\bar{\text{z}}/$$

The relationship between /fs/ and /v̄z̄/ is represented by the bar showing equivalence. In other words, /fs/ is identical to and equals /v̄z̄/; /vz/ without the bar is a voiced /fs/. In order to capture the fact that the forms {waivz} and {waifs} and {waif} are grammatically related, the descriptive linguist was generally limited to stating that {waif} is the singular form for a married female, {waivz} is the plural, and {waifs} is the possessive singular. Actually, describing these forms as morphologically complex was awkward.

The long component notion makes it possible to see that the relationship of /waifs/ and /waivz/ is one in which the final consonants agree in voicing, yet share their base form. /waif/ is composed of {waif} + {singular}, /waifs/ of {waif} + {possessive}, and /wàivz/ of {waif} + {plural}. According to Harris (1951:224), one may "group together into one morphophoneme the phonemes which replace each other in corresponding parts of the various members of a morpheme."

Morphophonemic symbols are devices which represent a class of phonemes whose members occur in a particular environment. /F/ is suggested as the symbol for the final consonant in the base form /waiF/. So written, the morpheme enclosed in slashes as in phonemic transcription but with a morphophonemic symbol becomes a base form having the allomorphs represented phonemically as /waif/ or /waiv/, depending on the phonological environment. That is, if /waiF/ occurs alone, it would be pronounced /waif/; if followed by the morpheme {plural}, it will be /waiv/; and if followed by the morpheme {possessive}, it will be /waif/.

Considering base forms allows the linguist to make "simple statements of variations within a series of morphemes" and "then the other allomorphs can be considered as resulting from describable changes from this base form under certain statable conditions." (Gleason 1961:82)

Changes under these "describable conditions" are called MORPHOPHONEMIC. Therefore, morphophonemics becomes the task of stating the changes which occur from a *base* to a *surface form*.

Morphophonemic alternations which involve relationships extracted as long components are often stated as morphophonemic rules.

$$/F/ \rightarrow \begin{bmatrix} /v/ \\ /f/ \end{bmatrix} / \begin{bmatrix} \underline{}\#/z/ \\ \underline{}\text{elsewhere} \end{bmatrix}$$

This is an early form of such a rule applying to the morpheme represented morphophonemically in its base form as /waiF/. The rule reads: the morphophoneme /F/ is realized as the phoneme /v/ when it occurs before a morpheme boundary (#) followed by the phoneme /z/. Everywhere else the /F/ shows up as /f/. Such rules which include morpheme boundaries are written in terms of distinctive features. Further, for English, this particular rule is one such that whenever /F/ is followed by a sound having the feature [+voice] the /F/ is realized as /v/. When this is stated, one is stressing the interrelatedness of features which co-occur in the sound system of English rather than extracting long components from linearly co-occurring phonemic entities. In the Jakobson and Halle framework one could state the rule as follows:

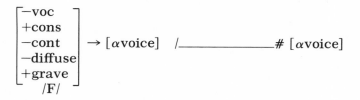

$$\begin{bmatrix} -\text{voc} \\ +\text{cons} \\ -\text{cont} \\ -\text{diffuse} \\ +\text{grave} \\ /F/ \end{bmatrix} \rightarrow [\alpha\text{voice}] \quad /\underline{\hspace{3cm}}\# [\alpha\text{voice}]$$

This rule states that a consonant which is a continuant, and made in the periphery of the mouth but forward (that is, /F/), adds to its set of simultaneously occurring sound features the feature of voicing when it occurs before a sound in which voicing is a distinctive feature. The symbol α *(alpha)* indicates that if the sound that /F/ appears before is a sound having the feature [+ voice], then the /F/ will add the feature [+voice] to its specifications in that environment and become /v/. If the /F/ occurs before a morpheme beginning with a sound with the feature [−voice], it will add the feature [−voice] to its specifications and occur as /f/.

Even though Harris sought to develop sophisticated methods for describing languages, he drifted along with the Europeans away from *parole* toward the analysis of *langue*. Of his own work on simultaneous features, Harris (1944, as in Joos 1963: 138) conceded

> It has been shown that this [type of] analysis creates a new set of elements out of the original allophones or phonemes, and that these elements have the same status as phonemes and are, indeed, merely generalized phonemes. Analysis into simultaneous parts is the only operation aside from segmentation into allophones that produces usable elements for descriptive linguistics.

Automata Theory and Context-Free Languages: Formalizing a Theory of Linguistic Structure

Earlier in this chapter we saw how the notion of language as a system, with a structure which could be described, gradually replaced the emphasis on language as describable speech in the work of some linguists. Building on these structural linguistic ideas, many linguists shifted toward "constructing a formalized general theory of linguistic structure" (Chomsky 1957; preface p. 5). While admitting the usefulness and productiveness of focusing on the best procedures for describing actual utterances as recorded in a field situation, linguists interested in fashioning a formal theory of language wished to stress that "a linguistic theory should not be identified with a manual of useful procedures, nor should it be expected to provide mechanical procedures for the discovery of grammars." (Chomsky 1957:55)

Noam Chomsky, in his *Syntactic Structures* (1957), proposed a theory of linguistic structure. He considered three possible theoretic models for linguistic structure:

a communication theory model,

a model incorporating immediate constituent analysis,

and a transformational model.

The innovative idea of a transformational structure in language amounted to a furthering of the ideas of European structuralism and also to an outgrowth of Harris's ideas from his "Co-occurrence and Transformations in Linguistic Structure." (*Language,* 1957:33) Specifically influential in the development of a transformational model of the theory of linguistic structure was Harris's observation that morphemes which occur together may share a component, just as phonemes which occur together may. Assuming that *la parole* and its description are the aims of linguistics, Harris (1951:373) believed that his method for describing language structure allowed the statement that

> . . .certain sequences of certain elements occur in the utterances of the language. This does not mean that other sequences of these elements, or other elements, do not occur; they may have occurred without entering into our records, or they may have not yet occurred in any utterance of the language, only to occur the next day. Aside from this, however, we may also be able to say that certain sequences almost never occur; we may know this from direct testing, or from the fact that the sequence goes counter to the most general regularities of our corpus.

Moreover:

> The work of analysis leads right up to the statements which
> enable anyone to synthesize or predict utterances in the
> language. These statements form a deductive system with
> axiomatically defined initial elements and with theorems
> concerning the relations among them. The final theorems
> would indicate the structure of the utterances of the language
> in terms of the preceding parts of the system.

Much of Chomsky's early work, especially his *Syntactic
Structures*, advanced these ideas. Harris actually went further toward anticipating a formal theory of language structure
by expressing the view that the structural system of a language might be presented

> . . . most boldly in an ordered set of statements defining the
> elements at each successive level or stating the sequences
> which occur at that level. Compactness, inspectability, and
> clarity of structure may be gained at various points by the use
> of symbols for class, variable member, and relation, or by the
> construction of geometric models (diagrams). (1951:373)

Mathematics was at a stage to be most helpful to the
linguists wishing to explore Harris's suggestion. During the
1950s automata theory received much attention. Many scholars saw the great breakthroughs in language translation
through the use of computers.

The possible theoretic models for a formalized description of
language examined by Chomsky in his *Syntactic Structures*
reflect the appeal of mathematical principles for the linguist in
the 1950s.

For the linguist wishing to describe the structural relationships among morphemes in a formal way, the grammar must
be finite even though the number of possible morpheme sequences is infinite.

The communication theoretic view is as follows:

> Suppose that we have a machine that can be in any one of a
> finite number of different internal states, and suppose that this
> machine switches from one state to another by producing a
> certain symbol (let us say an English word). One of these states
> is an *initial state;* another is a *final state.* Suppose that the ma-

> chine begins in the initial state, runs through a sequence of
> states (producing a word with each transition), and ends in the
> final state. Then we call the sequence of words that has been
> produced "a sentence." (Chomsky 1957:18–19).

This view, then, holds that such a machine defines a language as the set of sentences produced from the initial state to the final state. A machine defining a language this way automatically follows a sequence of operations programed into it. The set of sentences produced by the machine defines a FINITE STATE LANGUAGE, and the machine producing that set of sentences is called a FINITE STATE GRAMMAR. A finite state grammar may be extended by altering the operations the machine is programed to carry out. Figure 2–2 shows how a sentence is produced by tracing a path from "the initial point on the left to the final point on the right, always proceeding in the direction of the arrows." (1957:20)

However, a language thus defined requires a statement of what symbols are involved in sentence construction. Such a language can only produce what goes into it. As Chomsky observed, "it is *impossible,* not just difficult, to construct a device . . . which will produce all and only the grammatical sentences of English." (1957:21)

Requiring a formal theory of language structure, both at the phonological and syntactic level, to account for all and only the grammatical sentences of the language being described generated problems not encountered by the pre-Harris structuralists.

Harris anticipated this requirement of a formal theory by his observation that a grammar should consider the fact that certain sequences of morphemes not recorded in the body of speech data may occur "the next day." To him a description of the phonological and grammatical elements of a language ought to be generalizable. He pioneered the idea that one way this might be possible would be in the construction of a formal theory of linguistic structure.

However, the finite state grammar approach, though formal, could not accomplish this goal of producing *all* and *only* grammatical sentences of a language. Neither English nor any other natural language is a finite state grammar. Such finite state grammars fail to "explain or account for the ability of a

1. FINITE STATE GRAMMAR YIELDING THE SENTENCES
A. *The man comes*
B. *The men come*

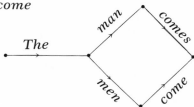

2. FINITE STATE GRAMMAR YIELDING INFINITE SENTENCES
A and B above plus other sentences such as
C. *The old man comes*
D. *The old men come*
E. *The old old man comes, etc.*

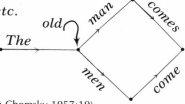

Figure 2-2. (Adapted from Chomsky 1957:19)

speaker of English to produce and understand new utterances, while he rejects other new sequences as not belonging to the language." (1957:23)

Linguists seeking a formal theory of language structure needed "a more powerful type of grammar and some more 'abstract' form of linguistic theory." (1957:24) The goal became one of constructing a formal grammar capable of producing or generating an infinite language. Much of the impetus for this came from the progress made in phonology where a universal and finite set of sound features in opposition were seen to underlie the infinite number of sound sequences in combination in the world's languages.

As noted in Chapter One, the descriptive linguist, upon the completion of phonemic analysis and then morphemic analysis, moved on to describing the syntax of the language represented in the body of speech data. IC analysis was the most widespread technique for such syntactic analysis. For example:

The man hit the ball.

The / man / hit / the / ball	single morphemes
The man / hit / the ball	subject/verb/object
The man / hit the ball	subject/predicate
The man hit the ball	sentence

Linguists from Harris on sought ways to state formally the relationships revealed by the mechanical procedure of IC analysis.

Following Harris to the letter as well as incorporating automata theoretical notions which transcended the finite state approach, Chomsky produced a restricted, yet more satisfying, theoretical model of language structure known as PHRASE STRUCTURE GRAMMAR. Actually he had reversed the procedure of IC analysis as Harris and Wells suggested by locating the formal criteria for breaking down utterances at successive stages. Certain notions of the processes involved in finite state grammars were useful here. One in particular was that of proceeding in the directions of the arrows from an initial to a final state. At the same time, however, the mechanical procedure of proceeding from left to right was modified. An example from Lyons (1970:98) underscores the inadequacy and subsequent rejection of the finite-state grammar approach for formally describing natural languages:

> It may not seem very plausible that anyone should seek to account for the production of an utterance such as *We have just been running* by saying that the speaker first selects *we* from the set of words permissible at the beginning of English sentences and then, having made their choice, selects *have*, as one of the words that has a certain probability of occurrence after *we*; then, having chosen *we* and *have*, selects *just* by virtue of its probability of occurrence after *we have*; and so on.

Advances in machine or automaton capability made it possible to refine the set of sentences which could be produced by a machine grammar so as to more closely approximate the nonfinite grammars of natural languages.

Both phrase structure and finite state grammars were ideas developed in work on computer language. In artifical or computer language, just as with natural languages, it is possible to generate nonfinite state languages. These are context-free languages.

The development and study of context-free languages through the devising of innovative automata or machine capabilities for defining sets of sentences in a nonfinite way became one of the concerns of computer specialists. According to Ginsberg (1966:viii),

> Of more than passing interest is the wedding of context-free languages and automata, each serving as a tool or source of problems for the other. In fact, . . . it is frequently difficult to decide if the subject is automata theory or language theory. As such, I view the subject matter of context-free languages as a logical succession to automata theory.

The subject matter of context-free languages is to a great extent the subject matter of early efforts to develop a formal theory of linguistic structure. The concept of a context-free as opposed to a finite-state language rested on the development of machines which could yield more than what was put into them.

For formal language theory, in the work of Chomsky both deterministic finite state automata (which yield finite state grammars) and the later developed pushdown automata (which yield context-free grammars) are significant.

Both types of machines act as recognition devices or acceptors:

> The first type, the *finite state acceptors,* yields the regular sets [that is, what goes in, comes out] . . . The second type, the *pushdown acceptors,* yields the languages. This provides a characterization of a language as a set which is accepted by some pushdown acceptor. (Ginsberg 1966:46)

As opposed to a finite state automaton acting as an acceptor, a pushdown acceptor has a finite number of states, a finite number of inputs, and a semi-infinite auxiliary tape (pushdown store).

The working tape capability marks the distinctive difference between a formal finite state and context-free grammar. To clarify what a semi-infinite auxiliary tape or pushdown store is, Ginsberg uses the analogy of a situation where one chooses a tray from a stack when entering a cafeteria line. The trays are stacked such that

1. Each time a new tray is inserted into the top of the stack, the trays underneath are pushed down against a spring;
2. the trays are used in reverse order to the order in which they are inserted into the stack — that is, first in — last out. (1966:60)

A context-free language, L, as defined by Chomsky, is not a finite state language "if and only if all the grammars that can be used to generate L are self-embedding." (Booth 1967:413)

Thus, a different type of machine is needed to generate the sentences of a context-free language than is needed for a finite state grammar. Such a machine is a phrase structure grammar in which

. . . the input and output tapes are the same, but the working tape [i.e., a read and write tape on which all of the intermediate calculations are accomplished] is restricted to be what is called a push-down tape or a push-down store. This tape can be written on, read from, or moved in either direction. As it moves from left to right past the reading head, however, all the tape locations on the right are left blank. Thus, if it is desired to read a symbol α to the left of the reading head, all of the symbols between α and the reading head are lost as α is moved under the head. Such an arrangement is described as "last in, first out" ordering. Machines that can be made to behave in this manner are called *push-down store automata*. (Booth 1967:392)

Figure 2–3 presents an early example of a phrase structure (henceforth, PS) grammar. Note that this grammar generates a number of sentences including *The man hit the ball* which was analyzed in IC terms above.

Rule i is read "rewrite Sentence as NP + VP." NP refers to noun phrase and VP to verb phrase. In contrast to finite state grammar, a PS grammar allows for certain elements to the left of the arrow to be rewritten again and again. Note that rule ii

(i)	Sentence	$\longrightarrow$	$NP + VP$
(ii)	NP	$\longrightarrow$	$T + N$
(iii)	VP	$\longrightarrow$	$Verb + NP$
(iv)	T	$\longrightarrow$	the
(v)	N	$\longrightarrow$	$man, ball$, etc.
(vi)	$Verb$	$\longrightarrow$	$hit, took$, etc.

Figure 2-3. A Simple Phrase Structure Grammar (Chomsky 1957:26)

expands NP to T + N and that a later rule (rule iii) expands VP to Verb + another NP. Within this framework rule ii can be applied until no more rules apply and the generated sentence results.

In order to derive the sentence *The man hit the ball*, one applies the six rules rewriting what is on the left of the arrow with what is on the right and then reading the rewritten form as input to another rule where it matches the left hand side of an arrow. For example, once rule iii has applied, then rule ii would apply again in order to expand the NP which resulted from the application of rule iii. After this, rules iv and v would again apply until the last line of the derivation yields a grammatical sentence. Figure 2–4 shows the derivation of the sentence *The man hit the ball*, using these phrase structure rules.

A PS grammar, then, is a finite set of initial strings and a finite

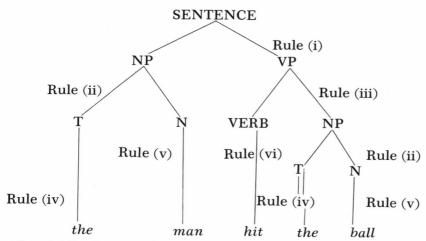

Figure 2-4. Tree Diagram of the Application of Rules in a Phrase Structure Grammar

set of rewrite rules. Systems of this form where initial strings are rewritten according to rewrite rules are also called TERMINAL LANGUAGES and include finite state languages but yield more complex natural language utterances.

Basically, PS grammar is a system of rewrite rules. It is context-free when the rewriting is done independently of the context in which the operation to be performed by the rule occurs. Rules i-vi above represent a context-free phrase structure grammar employing rewrite rules taking advantage of the pushdown store capacity of a machine in carrying out the rules. Such a grammar yields more natural language sentences than a finite state grammar can.

Still, with a PS grammar as a formal theory of language structure, the goal of generating all and only sentences of a language is not met.

From this point on in linguistics, we can see a divergence from an interest in describing the structure of particular languages to one in constructing a theory of language structure. The ideas in a phrase structure approach were the last ones from the Chomskian camp of immediate use to people dealing with describing the structure of bodies of data.

Syntactic Structures

By 1957, the year Chomsky's *Syntactic Structures* appeared, linguists tended to be either descriptive or theoretical in orientation. Maintaining both foci became difficult. The reason for this will be seen below in some of the ideas about the nature of a formal theory of language structure which would be more powerful than the PS model discussed above.

As stressed here, a PS grammar is closely related to the process used by descriptive linguists to describe sentences or utterances in a body of data through immediate constituent analysis. The PS model went beyond IC analysis in that it provided a formal way of segmenting parts of an utterance. Principles from automata theory were useful in making a PS grammar less arbitrary than descriptions of utterances in terms of immediate constituents.

However, to the linguist wishing a formal grammar to generate all and only sentences of a language, a grammar which could reproduce sentences from a limited sample of data only would not suffice. What was needed also was a way to place constraints on such a grammar so that ungrammatical utterances would not be generated while sentences never before uttered yet grammatical could be produced.

Furthermore, in the case of PS grammars, it was difficult to "define some order among the rules that produce these sentences" and to describe complex sentences. (Chomsky 1957: 35) Even when considering actual data, certain processes of natural languages such as conjunction could not be incorporated into the rules of a PS grammar. A grammar which could produce sentences such as S_3 *The scene of the movie and of the play was in Chicago* from the two simpler sentences S_1 *The scene of the movie was in Chicago* and S_2 *The scene of the play was in Chicago* would be more powerful than one based on a PS model.

Complex sentences of the nature of S_3 are formed thusly: $S_1 + S_2 \rightarrow S_3$. Forming S_3 requires more than the surface form of the input sentences S_1 and S_2. The phrase structures of those sentences must also be used. However, in a PS grammar, the past history of the input part of a rule is neither used nor needed.

> . . . each rule X → Y of the grammar [Σ, F] applies or fails to apply to a given string by virtue of the actual substance of this string. The question of how this string gradually assumed this form is irrelevant. If the string contains X as a substring, the rule X → Y can apply to it; if not the rule cannot apply. (1957:37)

In contrast, in order to generate complex sentences what is needed is a "more powerful machine, which can 'look back' to earlier strings in the derivation in order to determine how to produce the next step in the derivation." A theory which could handle such phenomena would involve "rules of a more complex type than those that correspond to a system of immediate constituent analysis." (1957:41)

The breakthrough in Chomsky's *Syntactic Structures* is his development of rules called GRAMMATICAL TRANSFORMATIONS. (1957:44)

development of rules called GRAMMATICAL TRANSFORMATIONS.
(1957:44)

> A grammatical transformation T operates on a given string
> (or . . . on a set of strings) with a given constituent structure
> and converts it into a new string with a new derived constitu-
> ent structure.

Transformational rules refer to the output of certain PS rules
and effect a change in their arrangement as constituents in
relation to each other.

The introduction of such rules as part of a formal theory of
the structure of language gave rise to the notion of TRANSFOR-
MATIONAL GRAMMAR, including within it a set of phrase structure rules.

> The transformational rules depend upon the previous applica-
> tion of the Phrase Structure rules and have the effect of not
> only converting one string of elements into another, but, in
> principle, of changing the associated phrase marker. (Lyons
> 1969:72)

Consider the sentence generated earlier by our PS grammar:
The man hit the ball. In this expanded theory of transformational (henceforth, T) grammar, such a sentence, which is the
result of the application of PS rules, is called a KERNEL SEN-
TENCE. T rules convert or transform kernel sentences into other
more complex sentences. Suppose one wished to generate the
sentence *The ball was hit by the man.* The PS rules cited earlier generate the kernel sentence, *The man hit the ball.* A T
rule is composed of the kernel sentence's structural description
(this marks the input string) and its structural change (this
marks the change needed to derive the transformed string
from the string defined in the structural description).

The structural description (SD)[3] *The man hit the ball is*

$$\text{SD: } NP_1 - V - NP_2$$

This is the input for the passive transformation. The structural change (SC) required in order to transform *The man hit the ball* to *The ball was hit by the man* is:

$$\text{SC: } X_1 - X_2 - X_3 \Rightarrow X_3 - be + en - X_2 - by + X_1$$

That is:

	The man	/	*hit*	/	*the ball*
	X_1		X_2		X_3
SD:	NP_1		V		NP_2

	The ball	/	*was*	/	*hit*	/	*by*	/	*the man*
	X_3		be+en		X_2		by		X_1
SC:	NP_2				V				NP_1

> The passive transformation involves three operations: 1) Subject and object NP switch positions; 2) *by-* is prefixed to the original subject NP in its new position; 3) *be + en* (that is, the auxiliary verb *be* + past tense) is inserted before the verb. (Southworth and Daswani 1974:162)

Note that the structural description which is the input to a T rule requires returning to nonterminal symbols in the phrase structure of the kernel sentence. When NP_1 is transformed, it is transformed along with the PS rules yet to follow which then apply after the T rule has applied.

Further, T grammar as introduced by Chomsky was considered to be a more powerful formal model for the description of language structure because, in addition to handling complexity beyond the scope of a PS grammar in a more satisfactory way, it also "could account more satisfactorily for certain types of structural ambiguity." An illustration of this point is the sentence *Flying planes can be dangerous.* Lyons (1969:84–85) summarizes the example as follows:

> . . . a sentence like *Flying planes can be dangerous* is ambiguous (cf., *To fly planes can be dangerous* and *Planes which are flying can be dangerous*); and yet, under both interpretations, the immediate constituent analysis is, presumably,

(((flying) (planes)) (((can) (be)) (dangerous))) . . . It would be possible to generate a sentence like *Flying planes can be dangerous* within a phrase structure grammar and to assign to it two different phrase markers—differing with respect to the labels assigned to the node dominating *flying*. But this would not be an intuitively satisfying account of the ambiguity; and it would fail to relate the phrase *flying planes*, on the one hand, to *planes which are flying*, and on the other hand, to *someone flies planes*. The transformational analysis accounts for the ambiguity by relating two different underlying strings (let us say, *plane + s + be + ing + fly* and *someone + fly + plane + s*) to the same derived string.

This example of the passive transformation shows how an OBLIGATORY TRANSFORMATION in a transformational grammar works. The handling of the different possible readings of the ambiguous sentence *Flying planes can be dangerous* illustrates the use of OPTIONAL TRANSFORMATIONS.

The idea of optional transformations and of being able to analyze sentences which may be understood in more than one way is the step which moves the search for a formal theory of linguistic structure away from the goal of describing languages as utterances in a body of elicited data.

In *Syntactic Structures*, Chomsky advanced the idea that

> To understand a sentence it is necessary to reconstruct its representation on each level, including the transformational level where the kernel sentences underlying a given sentence can be thought of, in a sence [sic], as the "elementary content elements" out of which this sentence is constructed. In other words, one result of the formal study of grammatical structure is that a syntactic framework is brought to light which can support semantic analysis. (1957:168)

With these words, the techniques of Bloomfield and Gleason became part of the field of language description.

By way of a conclusion, we will summarize the model of language structure as a whole by incorporating the T grammar of *Syntactic Structures*. Here is how a formal theory of the structure of language looked in 1957:

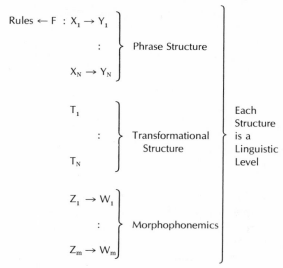

Σ : Sentence :

Rules ← F : $X_1 \rightarrow Y_1$

:   } Phrase Structure

$X_N \rightarrow Y_N$

T_1

:   } Transformational Structure

T_N

$Z_1 \rightarrow W_1$

:   } Morphophonemics

$Z_m \rightarrow W_m$

Each Structure is a Linguistic Level

Figure 2-5.   The Structure of Language: 1957 (Adapted from Chomsky 1957:46)

The way this formal grammar works is by constructing derivations beginning with *sentence* as a given and running through:

1. the rules of F (the PS) which yield "a terminal string that will be a sequence of morphemes, though not necessarily in the correct order" (1957:46).   For example, *The + man + past + hit + the + ball* + passive

2. the rules of T (the sequences of transformations). For example, *The + man* + past + *hit + the + ball* + passive ⇒ *The + ball* + passive + past + *hit* + (agent) + *the + man*

3. the rules of the morphophonemic structure (level). For example, [ðə + bal + wəz + hIt + bai + ðə + mæn]

Hence, a generated sentence.

A grammar in the syntactic structures framework consists of three sets of rules at three linguistic levels (see the phonemic, morphemic, and syntactic levels of descriptive linguistics).

The PS rules, T rules, and morphophonemic rules all interrelate in a language system. Morphophonemic rules, remember, involve assigning the correct phonological shape to morphemes in particular environments.

> Order of rules is essential, and in a properly formulated grammar it would be indicated in all three sections along with a distinction between optional and obligatory rules and, at least in the transformational part, a statement of conditional dependence among rules. The result of applying all of these rules is an extended derivation terminating in a string of phonemes of the language under analysis, i.e., a grammatical utterance. (1957:114)

A T grammar's morphophonemic level contains rules much as those developed in the Harris framework discussed earlier in this chapter. Syntactic structures, then, essentially by evolving from a phrase structure approach, extended Harris's ideas beyond the morphophonemic to the syntactic level. This science of linguistics which emerged from structuralism involved describing sentences in terms of sets of rules relating grammatical categories such as NP and VP, and so on to each other and then relating the elements of a sentence – again through a set of rules – to its phonological shape.

Summary

Structural linguistics evolved from descriptive linguistics. It emerged as a field with the aim of constructing a comprehensive theory of the hierarchical system of units constituting the expressive side of language. The description of levels of speech structure necessarily reached a point where the expression of speech could not be analyzed without reference to content. Content could not be mechanically analyzed in terms of units of structure at various descriptive levels as amenably as expression could be. So, some scholars involved in the study of language suggested that the concern of the field might shift from speech as the data source to the shared system of sound and grammatical relationships within languages that underlie speech. The impetus for this came from essentially two major influences:

1. DeSaussure's distinction between *la langue* (the system of a language) and *la parole* (the spoken utterances of a language)

2. The Prague linguists' contribution of systematic phonology. That is, the notion that the phonemes isolatable as units in a stream of speech *(la parole)* are made up of sound features which are related to each other as binary oppositions in the language's structured phonological system *(la langue)*.

Structuralists felt that if the sound system of the structure of language could be formally stated by describing the relationships among sound features in opposition, then it would also be possible to state the grammatical and meaningful structure of *langue* as well.

The structural linguist's move away from describing speech data in favor of attempts to explain the systematic nature of a particular language exemplified by instances of speech resulted largely because descriptive linguists had come to agree "in principle that the most desirable kind of linguistic description is a *formal description*." (Dinneen 1967:359) Harris (1951:18), a chief proponent of this view, defined the distinction between his ideas and the practice of descriptive linguistics this way:

> For the linguist [that is, the descriptivist], analyzing a limited corpus consisting of just so many bits of talking which he has heard, the element X is thus associated with an extensionally defined class consisting of so many features in so many of the speech occurrences in his corpus. However, when the linguist [that is, the structuralist] offers his result as a system representing the language as a whole, he is predicting that the elements set up for his corpus will satisfy all other bits of talking in that language. The element X then becomes associated with an intensionally defined class consisting of such features of any utterance as differ from other features, or relate to other features, in such and such a way.

The structuralist approach saw the task of the linguist to have changed from describing what the elements of transcribed speech are to one of describing what relationships underlie all instances of speech in a particular language.

Agreeing with this view of the task of linguistics, Chomsky, in developing the needed approach for analyzing the syntactic level of a language's structure, felt that it is not sufficient for a grammar to describe a set of observed sentences. A grammar should produce all the grammatical sentences of a language.

In order to write a grammar which could describe the system of a language in terms of its phonological, morphological, and syntactic structure, the idea developed that if a grammar could be designed which could produce grammatical sentences, the processes used would constitute a grammar. Further, such a sentence-producing grammar would constitute a formal theory of the structure of language. In the emerging field of computer technology formal devices for producing computer languages were simultaneously being developed. This provided a model upon which the notion of a sentence-producing grammar as a theory of the structure of natural language could be built. If sentences could be produced, the phonological, morphological, and syntactic rules or processes upon which they were produced could be said to constitute a model of syntactic structure.

The view of grammar which the structuralist ideas advanced in linguistics culminated in Chomsky's notions of grammar presented in *Syntactic Structures* (1957). Grammar was held to be

> . . .a device of some sort for producing all of the grammatical, and none of the ungrammatical, sentences of a language. Such a grammar usually contains several linguistic "levels," for example, phonemics, morphology, and phrase structure." (Dinneen 1967:360)

A major shift from structuralism, as guiding the development of a theory of language structure, to Chomsky's later transformational/generative grammar, as a theory of language, was a change in the structural object of the theory. In *Syntactic Structures*, Chomsky as a structuralist proposed a device for producing the structure of *langue* (a particular language's structured system composed of phonological morphological and syntactic levels). In later formulations, a grammar as a theory of language structure is a device for producing the structure of *competence* (the knowledge of language structure speakers of any and all languages have). As we saw the object of analysis in the science of language to differ from a particular language as speech *(la parole)* to structure *(la langue)* in descriptivism and structuralism respectively; we will also see a shift as well in the object of analysis from a particular language's structure *(la langue)* to the universal or general structure of knowledge that humans share which allows them to produce and understand sentences (competence) in transformational grammar.

With the development of the idea that linguistics ought to be concerned with formalizing the structure of languages and thereby develop a theory of language, the question arose regarding the adequacies and inadequacies of theoretical formulations. Throughout the science of the study of language, whether as linguistic theory or language description, the need for evaluating the product (a description of data or a formal structural sentence-producing device) has been addressed. Now that we have looked at descriptive linguistics as the basis of later models of language description and structural linguistic theory, we will consider some of the issues involved in determining what makes a description adequate and what constitutes an adequate theory.

For Thought and Discussion

1. What was the major emphasis of structural linguistics as compared to descriptive linguistics? How would a structuralist view the following data: a certain language has three nasals, /m/ /n/ /ŋ/ and three voiceless stops, /p/ /t/ /k/; the only combinations which are possible of these six are /mp/, /nt/, and /ŋk/. How would a descriptive linguist view the same data?

2. What did deSaussure mean by *la parole,* by *la langue?* Would you say descriptive linguists were concerned with *la parole* or *la langue?* Explain your answer.

3. In the word /bɪt/ in English, /b/ is said to be in paradigmatic relationship with /p/, why? With what phoneme is /t/ in paradigmatic relationship? What is the distinctive feature which differentiates the two sounds /b/ and /p/? How does *paradigmatic relationship* differ from *syntagmatic relationship?*

4. Returning to question 1 and the combinations /mp/, /nt/, and /ŋk/, what generalization can be made about the co-occurrence of a voiceless stop and a nasal in English?

5. How would a linguist like Harris relate the "words" *wreath*

and *wreaths* whose phonetic representations are /riyθ/ and /riyðz/ respectively? What would be the base form of the word *wreath*?

6. Harris wanted to be able to make predictions about the sequence of segments in a language: for example, where the sequence /sp/ occurs but /sb/ does not, /zb/ occurs but not /zp/. Looking at language on a higher level and breaking down a sentence into the component parts (noun phrase, auxiliary, and verb phrase), what can be said about their sequence in a normal statement in English such as *Mary is reading a book on linguistics* where *Mary* = NP, *is* = AUX (or tense), and *reading a book on linguistics* = VP?

7. Think of the answer to question 6 as a base form for a sentence. Then consider for a moment the example of [waif] and [waivz] where [waiF] is taken to be the base form, with /F/ realized as [v] in [waivz] in the surface form when /F/ is followed by the plural morpheme /z/. Set up a parallel relation between the base form of the sentence in question 6 and its surface realization as the question, *Is Mary reading a book on linguistics?*

8. Which of the two sentences *Mary is reading a book* and *Is Mary reading a book?* is generated by the phrase-structure rules? How would Chomsky show the relationship between these two sentences?

NOTES

[1]Descriptive linguistics emphasized synchronic versus diachronic studies and stressed that the only valid comparisons of languages were those involving descriptions of languages done at similar time states and based on rigorous descriptive procedures. Most traditional general linguistic texts contained a statement much to the effect that it is customary to distinguish two major divisions of linguistic study, known as *descriptive* (or *synchronic*) *linguistics,* and *historical* (or *diachronic*) *linguistics.* Since it is the task of this volume to articulate a recently evolved distinction between linguistic theory and language description with structuralism as the catalyst, our position is that descriptive and historical linguistics are part of language description while linguistic theory seeks to explain the nature of language.

In this chapter, certain linguists figure as particularly important in the developments shaping the growth of the scientific study of language. Here, we present brief biographical data on the major figures whose ideas we have widely quoted.

H. A. Gleason is best known as the author of *An Introduction to Descriptive Linguistics* (1955, rev. ed. 1961). Gleason's work is an explicit account of the procedures for describing a body of linguistic data as composed of features of spoken language phonetically transcribed. Gleason presents methods which provide a rigorous way to segment speech into units at hierarchically arranged levels of structure. Each descriptive level of speech (phonemic, morphemic, syntactic) must be described separately according to the procedures. The goal is an analysis of a body of data as representing the structure of linguistic expression. The work of Gleason carries on many of the ideas of Bloomfield (1933) and presents the most useful and practical approach to describing speech. Efforts to refine the methods of descriptive linguistics by other scholars had shifted the field from a focus on speech *(parole)* to a focus on the analysis of linguistic structure as a system of relationships among units. DeSaussure, Harris, and Chomsky, through such efforts to refine descriptive linguistics, were important in this shift.

Ferdinand deSaussure, a synchronic structural linguist, is best known for his *Cours de Linguistique Général (General Linguistics Course)* published in 1916. This is a book of his university lectures assembled from notes and outlines by his students after his death in 1913. DeSaussure shifted the goal of linguistics from a focus on the structure of expression to a focus on the structure of a linguistic system — that is, he moved the field from a concern with *la parole* to a position of concern now exclusively with *la langue.* The analysis of *la parole*, or more expressly of speech, remained the concern solely of descriptive linguistics while this structuralist approach looked at *la langue.* DeSaussure is said to have had three objectives for his work: 1) to see that the synchronic study of language becomes a science, 2) to demonstrate in a scientific study of language that there are linguistic facts, 3) to set up procedures for identifying and analyzing linguistic facts. As we see in this chapter, the distinctions of *la langue* and *la parole*, of synchronic and diachronic language study, of paradigmatic and syntagmatic relations stem from his efforts to develop a linguistic science.

Zellig Harris envisioned structural linguistics in his book by that title (1951) as a field centering on devising "structural methods for descriptive linguistics." (v) To Harris, the analysis resulting from his methods is a description of language as an analyzable system of relatable elements. Harris's intention for what he called structural linguistics was that it be a refinement of the descriptive linguistics he knew (essentially the Bloomfieldian approach). Harris was influenced by some of deSaussure's ideas which marked his approach, as a result, as a departure from descriptive linguistics. His methods for describing linguistic data, as distinct from descriptive linguistics and in accord with deSaussure's views, saw synchronic study as primary, considered the object of description to be the underlying system of language rather than its manifestation in speech or expression, and attempted to describe the relationships among linguistic entities as well as the entities themselves. In this chapter, the concepts of the morphophoneme, the notion of components (as forerunners of distinctive features), and the suggestion that the analysis of linguistic structure might begin with utterances rather than move up to them from lower "levels" of analysis in progressive discrete stages, were developed by Harris as useful analytic tools for describing the linguistic system represented by a body of data. To describe the structure that surface synchronic data represents (rather than describing the data itself), Harris felt, would make it possible to predict further utterances in the language beyond the sample under analysis. To him, such a description forms "a deductive system with axiomatically defined initial elements and with theorems concerning the relations among them. The final theorems would indicate the structure of the utterances of the language in terms of the preceding parts of the system." (1951:372–73)

As deSaussure asked that the study of language become scientific and defined its parameters, Harris responded by providing methods to formally analyze its system.

Noam Chomsky is best known as the founder of transformational/generative grammar which in the context of this discussion represents the end result of the shift from describing expression (descriptive linguistics) to describing underlying linguistic structure (structural linguistics). Chomsky was a student of Zellig Harris and adopted Harris's views regarding the desirability of formalizing linguistic description and of focusing on stating relationships within a linguistic system. Where descriptive linguists analyze expression (speech) and structuralists examine *la langue* and not *la parole*, transformationalists again shifted the focus of the field. In *Syntactic Structures* (1957), Chomsky attempted to refine the analysis of *la langue*. We will see in other chapters that in later works, Chomsky too, as Harris and deSaussure had done, to accomplish his goals shifted the object of linguistic study—this time away from *la langue* to what he calls *competence*. In Chapter 2, the ideas of Chomsky have been seen mainly as they developed in response to the work of deSaussure and Harris and were later influenced by developments in work with computers calling for a scientific way to describe a linguistic system rather than a procedural approach to describing actual speech.

Chomsky's ideas in this chapter represent the earliest formulation of transformational/generative grammar. As we will see in later chapters, he has since abandoned some of his own notions (e.g., kernel sentences) and changed the theory itself. *Syntactic Structures* considers *la langue* still to be the object of study. In formulations of Chomsky's theory since, he intends the theory to account for what he now calls *competence* or generalized linguistic knowledge as distinct from *la langue*. In attempting to be a better structuralist, Chomsky was led to develop his own transformationalist school. Harris, influenced by deSaussure, in an effort to do better descriptive linguistics became a structuralist.

[2]The * preceding *|sbIn| follows the convention of using the asterisk to denote an unattested, nonoccurring or hypothetical form. Such forms are called *starred* forms.

[3]Note that the sentence *The man hit the ball* actually has the SD: $NP_1 - AUX - V - NP_2$

(*the man*) (past tense) (*hit*) (*the ball*)

However, Chomsky's example of a simple PS grammar omits the use of AUX to represent the tense marker. For clarity of exposition and consistency, it is also omitted in our example of the passive as a transformational rule.

THREE

Adequacy of Linguistic Description

Descriptive linguists disagree on how analyses of their speech data should be presented. Some present their language descriptions on an item and arrangement (henceforth, IA) model; others use an item and process (henceforth, IP) model.

Gleason (1961:214–215) characterizes the debate on the merits of each descriptive model this way:

> One fundamental cleavage between different types of descriptive statement rests in the entities which are made the basis of description. . .Structure is described in terms of elements of various sorts, morphemes, words, phrases, etc. and the arrangements in which they are joined. Thus the English past verb is described as a construction of a verb stem (e.g., *walk*) plus an affix, {−D,}, which in this particular case is pronounced /−t/ and spelled − ed. Every statement in one kind of descriptive grammar would be of the same general form. Each construction is described as composed of two or more

elements, each usually specified as any member of a certain constituent class (in the example just cited, "verb stem"). This technique may be called the *element model*.

A second basis for description is the *process model*. This must also start from elements, to be sure, but typically the statement is in terms of one element and one process. Thus the English past verb might be described as resulting from the application of a process (perhaps acceptably labeled as "preterization," or something of the sort) to a verb. With an example like *walked* this seems a bit awkward: nothing seems to be gained by describing *walked* as *walk* having undergone preterization, which in this instance takes the special form of suffixation. But with an example like *ran*, the impression is more favorable: this seems quite appropriately described as *run* having undergone a process of preterization, which in this instance takes the form of vowel change. The process model seems more satisfying than an element model for words like *ran;* and indeed the element model is necessarily stretched in some barely satisfactory way to cover such cases at all.

The descriptivist must represent the levels of language as speech. The structuralist must describe what it is that members of a speech community share. The transformationalist must explain the rules accounting for the human knowledge which permits language acquisition. This is done by formulating rules which express language competence. An adequate description of speech or of the knowledge involved in understanding sentences or acquiring language presupposes that each task may be evaluated by a set of criteria for determining an adequate description vis-à-vis the goals of each task.

Descriptive accounts of speech data are considered adequate to the extent that they represent the observed (transcribed) speech. Structural descriptions of *la langue* are adequate to the extent that they are generalizations about the linguistic system being described. Competent transformational/generative descriptions are adequate to the extent that they allow grammars representing the intuitions of speakers of the world's languages to be selected.

One way to consider what is at issue regarding the notion of adequacy in the study of language is to frame the main points in what may be called the principle of three adequacies (Eastman 1975:24), which involves stating the goals of linguistics regardless of the theoretical or methodological analysis.

According to Chomsky (1964:923–24), an observationally adequate grammar is one which displays the data. A descriptively adequate grammar is one which accounts for *all* sentences of a language and *only* the sentences of that language. Finally, *explanatory adequacy*, a theoretical rather than a grammatical goal, aims to provide a principled basis, independent of any particular language, for the selection of the descriptively adequate grammar of language.

Descriptive Adequacy/External versus Internal

To Chomsky (1964:923), a descriptively adequate grammar provides a "correct account of the linguistic intuition of the native speaker." To the descriptive linguist, a grammar is an inventory of linguistic elements and classes derived from the analysis of strings of transcribed speech data elicited from a native speaker. Descriptive linguistics prohibits attempts to describe native speaker intuitions. *The* native speaker embodies a shared system of linguistic elements; *a* native speaker expresses it. Therefore, to evaluate descriptive linguistics using criteria of descriptive adequacy makes little sense.

External Descriptive Adequacy and Structural Linguistics

In the earlier discussion of Zellig Harris's structural linguistics, we saw that, although Harris aimed to develop better methods for using the ideas of the base form, the morphophoneme and the long component, he also moved away from describing *la parole* and toward analyzing *la langue*.

As we pointed out in Chapter Two, the linguistic theory of the Prague School focused on the way language used sound matter. Prague structuralists held that any individual speaker of a language has "adequate command of his own mother tongue which he is able to use in the more or less differentiated situations he faces in his daily life." Moreover, "such adequate command may be taken as evidence for what the Prague groups terms 'linguistic consciousness' (and what is roughly comparable to N. Chomsky's 'intuition')." (Vachek, 1972:25)

The Prague School contended that this linguistic consciousness that their theory sought to describe "appears to be the only safe ground on which the teaching of a foreign language can build." *(ibid.)* The idea is that a student can be taught a language which he can use in the same "more or less differentiated situations he faces in his daily life" in which he uses his native language. The theory and practice of language teaching derived from the Prague School offered the possibility

> of comparing any two languages, whether generically related or not, and, on top of this, two different stages of one and the same language. In effecting such comparison, common background. . . is constituted by the communicative needs and wants to be expressed, which are roughly analogous in all language communities. Then, of course, the different ways in which the compared languages express these needs and wants are mutually compared to make the specific features of the given languages stand out as clearly as possible. (Vachek 1972:24)

In addition to the structural linguistics of Harris and of the Prague School. Another school of linguistic theory based in Copenhagen advanced another structuralist theory of language known as GLOSSEMATICS.

This theoretical approach also had its roots in the Saussurean distinctions of *la langue* and *la parole*, synchronic and dischronic. Interestingly, many of the works dealing with how one might evaluate a structural analysis of a language as adequate derived from this particular school.

In 1950, Einar Haugen, as president of the Linguistic Society of Chicago, delivered an address entitled "Directions in Modern Linguistics." In it, he surveyed the field of linguistics at that time as a meld of the European and American postdescriptive (post-Bloomfieldian) schools. Many of the points he made involve comparing the approach of the advocates of glossematics with that of Harris's followers.

A main point he emphasized is that with structural linguistics there developed a METALANGUAGE in the field of linguistics.

New terms have been created whose purpose is to make research techniques explicit, so that we may talk not merely about language, but also about how to talk about language. Among logicians it has become standard practice to refer to such a terminology as a *metalanguage,* which is defined as a language which is used to make assertions about another language. (Haugen, 1951:358 in Joos, ed. *Readings in Linguistics*)

Haugen applied yet another term, METALINGUISTICS, "to the kind of research that has brought forth such new terms as *phone, morph, substitution, constituent, focus class,* and *tactics" (ibid.).* Metalinguists, Haugen claimed, employ such terms. The different schools of linguistics were characterized by different metalanguages. For example, the Americans used terms largely from Harris's approach. The Europeans used terms incorporated into the glossematic approach which was an outgrowth of the works of deSaussure, Trubetzkoy, and others. In an amusing paragraph, Haugen asserted:

It is not my purpose to present an analysis of Hjelmslev's theory [Hjelmslev was the leader of the glossematic school] nor an evaluation of its associated procedures. I merely wish to point out that in Europe a new metalanguage is being shaped which is at least as different from that of our school grammars as is the American metalanguage. The two are as mutually incomprehensible as French and English, and we shall soon need a bimetalingual lexicon to translate from one to the other. We are reaching a point where the metalanguage of linguistics is falling apart into metadialects, jeopardizing the unity of our science. Even among American metalinguists we note the rise of what may be called meta-idiolects, which makes it confusing to follow recent discussion. Whatever differences of emphasis and approach there may be between the American and European schools, it is my conclusion after making an effort to assimilate the leading features of each that they are talking about the same thing and struggling toward the same goal. *(ibid.)*

The goal of structural linguistics, then, was to provide an adequate theory and method to use in describing the *langue* of various languages. Evaluation procedures involve measuring each structuralist "school" against the other to try to decide which set of discovery procedures would yield the best accounts of the knowledge shared by members of speech communities. The approach judged best could be considered more descriptively adequate with respect to the other approaches.

Contending that the European and American schools were "talking about the same thing," Haugen made the following comparison.

American (Haugen)	European (Hjelmslev)
1. There should be a "mathematical" syntax.	1. There should be a linguistic algebra.
2. Structural analyses are formal.	2. Glossematics is based on "an exclusively formal set of postulates."
3. A metalanguage needs to be developed to apply to the analysis of the structure of every language.	3. A metalanguage needs to be developed to apply to the analysis of the structure of every language.
4. Utterances should be broken down through IC analysis into a. constituents b. focus class c. sequence class.	4. Utterances should be broken down into constituents using the deductive method into a. derivates b. paradigms c. chains.
5. Constituents are analyzed through substitution.	5. Constituents are analyzed through commutation.

Both substitution and commutation are procedures whereby one attempts to "replace any part of an utterance with other linguistic material" in order "to determine whether the utterance is divisible and how best to divide it." (Haugen 1951:359)

Throughout twentieth-century linguistics, descriptive, structural, and transformational linguists have debated which approach was best, often failing to consider that each group had different goals. Evaluating the approaches by comparing them makes no sense; comparing competing models within a single approach does. Since Haugen's presidential address in 1950, another word has come into prominence in general linguistics which applies to situations where evaluation procedures cannot determine whether one approach is more descriptively adequate than another. If two types of analysis appear equal in how well they describe the *langue* of particular languages, they are said to be NOTATIONAL VARIANTS of each other.

Even within the various structuralist schools, there were competing models of grammatical description, each with proponents claiming that their scheme was more adequate than others. Since our point here is to demonstrate the significance of criteria of adequacy in the study of linguistics and language description, it is sufficient to mention some of the competing approaches within American structural linguistics which vied with Zellig Harris's approach.* Many scholars were convinced that these were each notational variants of the others.

In attempting to decide which approach among the American or the European schools "best" encompasses the language system shared by a community of speakers, we will return to Haugen's address on the state of the art in the early 1950s.

In his view, structural linguistics unfairly sold descriptive linguistics short: both ought to complement each other in order to lay the groundwork for an "adequate" linguistics. But differing goals of description made unifying the existing approaches difficult, if not impossible. Outlining what he thought to be the advantages of mathematical linguistics (structural) over traditional linguistics (descriptive), Haugen held that

> . . . traditional linguistics has sought objectivity by adopting an external standard to which the language may be referred, while present-day linguistics seeks to find internal, relational standards; and finally, that while the internal or distributional

*The reader wishing to compare the schemes in more detail is referred to a 1964 monograph by Paul Postal, *Constituent Structure: A Study of Contemporary Models of Syntactic Description,* as well as to analyses done under each framework specifically. Some of the major approaches to analyzing the structure of an utterance which were and are prevalent in America are:
1. Bernard Bloch's approach to the analysis of Japanese syntax
2. Rulon Wells's immediate constituent analysis
3. Zellig Harris's morpheme class substitution system
4. Charles Hockett's item and arrangement system
5. Sydney Lamb's stratificational syntax
6. Kenneth Pike's tagmemics
7. Charles Hockett's constructional grammar
8. Zellig Harris's string analysis
9. Noam Chomsky's phrase structure grammar

standards may lead to useful discoveries concerning the internal organization or structure of the language, linguistics cannot, unless it wishes to become entirely circular or mathematical, afford to reject the use of external standards to give its relational data concrete validity in the real world. (1951: 359)

A major criticism of the structuralists by descriptivists is that the former are more interested in "contributing more to elegance than to learning." The descriptivists insist on linking linguistic relationships to concrete sense data. They generally do not recognize the virtue of economy in mathematical descriptions as advocated by the structuralists. Descriptivists see no point in structural analyses of *la langue* which cannot be related to *la parole*. The structuralist analysis of *la langue* which admittedly presupposes "a characterization of all the utterances of a language" (1951:363) involves the adoption of "arbitrary and unsupported principles of analysis, more characterized by esthetic than by scientific validity." (*ibid.*) Haugen (1951:363) observed that the "metalinguist (i e. structuralist) and the physical linguist (i.e. descriptivist) would necessarily need to learn to maintain a cooperative working relationship if they wished to establish linguistic analyses which would not be circular and which would be testable as valid in the real world." It is this point which makes the approaches irreconcilable since structuralists did not expect linguistic systems to have real world validity. They seek to describe what a community of speakers have as an unconscious knowledge of their particular language (*la langue*) and not what each speaker speaks (*la parole*) in a real world setting.

The structuralists believe that the most descriptively adequate characterization of this knowledge would make use of mathematical principles and would be evaluatable in terms of economy. This criterion of evaluating structural analyses of *la langue* is known in the linguistic literature as the SIMPLICITY CRITERION, a measure whereby notational variants could be judged with respect to each other with the most concise analysis as long as each analysis being compared accounted for the data.

The purpose of linguistics, so maintained most scholars, was to produce descriptions of languages. But confusion developed over what should be described as *la parole* (descriptivist position) or *la langue* (structuralist position). The mathematically oriented people were structuralists who tended toward economy of description, thereby making many descriptions unintelligible for nonstructuralists. Haugen (1951:363) charged that structuralist descriptions bristled "like a page of symbolic logic," lacking "the leisurely, even charming quality of traditional grammar." Moreover, "Economy may not always be a virtue; in some cases it results from poverty, and . . . it must be replaced by an expansion into real sounds and real meaning whenever it is put to any practical use." The "best" kind of analysis is determined by extralinguistic goals.

> But in giving us a metalanguage with which to talk about various kinds of analysis, and in thereby enabling us to point out where the analyses of the past have differed or fallen by the wayside, the metalinguists [i.e., structuralists] have done us a real service . . . Whatever the metalanguage used, the goal of our investigation is the structure of the language used by actual speakers. Whatever we may mean by structure, the one thing we can be sure of is that it is no more like the language itself than the botanist's description of an apple is like an apple. You can't eat the botanist's description and you can't talk the linguist's description. But once the apple or the language comes before your eye, a good description will make it possible to identify it and even predict some few of its major sensory features.

Simplicity

The advent of PS grammar and the early stages of grammar as an approach to describing languages brought to the fore the notion of simplicity as a means of deciding among competing analyses which is more descriptively adequate. Bach outlined the state of linguistics in the 1960s much as Haugen did for the 1950s. According to Bach (1964:178):

> Two grammars for the same language might be equally com-
> plete and correct, and we wish our general theory to provide a
> criterion of choice between them. Of two theories that cover
> the same facts, it is usual to choose that one which is simpler
> (or more economical). It seems natural to identify simplicity
> with the number of symbol tokens [i.e., occurrences of sym-
> bols] in the grammar. We would exclude from our count sym-
> bols of the metatheory . . . and count as single symbols
> whatever appears between these signs, i.e., the primes of the
> various parts of the grammar.

Bach illustrates the use of the simplicity measure with a
case from phonology. Given a language description having bilabial, velar, and alveolar initial aspirated stops (p^h, k^h, t^h) and
three final unaspirated stops with the same points of articulation respectively (p, k, t), a description stating that there is a
stop series in the language (/p/, /k/, /t/) where there are three
stop phonemes with similar patterns of distribution is more
economical than a description stating the allophonic variation
for each phoneme separately. The simplicity measure afforded
a way to be less dependent on the discovery procedures which
the descriptivists and early structuralists depended upon. It
allowed judgments to be made as to the adequacy of a description based on the economy of the whole description.

> Generally, since grammatical theories, like other theories, are
> never complete, a new theory will be merely simpler that [sic]
> the one it is intended to replace. It will account for new facts
> as well or will be more correct in the sense that it excludes
> certain nonsentences generated by the other theory or ex-
> plains better certain connections between sentences, and so
> on. (Bach, 1964:179)

Later Chomsky, in discussing evaluation procedures in general, stated that a grammar can be justified on external
grounds of descriptive adequacy *if it states the facts* about the
language correctly. Furthermore, "In the case of a linguistic
theory that is merely descriptive, only one kind of justification
can be given—namely, we can show that it permits grammars
to meet the external conditions of descriptive adequacy."

(1965:41). The question is one of evaluating competing grammars not vis-à-vis each other but rather in terms of a general linguistic theory. Structuralism, descriptivism, and transformationalism are each proposed as general linguistic theories. It is a different question to choose among the competing theories of language than it is to choose among competing analyses within each theoretical framework.

Within the theory developed by Chomsky, simplicity was proposed as a way to evaluate competing grammars within that theory and based on that model. The choice among competing grammars must be able to be made from the theory itself.

Observational Adequacy

For each type of adequacy discussed so far, we see a clear relationship between the goals of the description and the criteria for determining its adequacy. Since observational adequacy is concerned with presenting linguistic data in the best manner given the analyses of the body into isolatable units, that is why it is the primary goal of the descriptive linguist. To the structuralists and transformationalists it is desirable, not paramount, because their body descriptive adequacy criteria are more important in evaluation than are observational criteria. For the descriptive linguist, observational adequacy criteria provide evaluation measures to be used in deciding among descriptions of data. Here simplest is not necessarily best.

Goals of Describing a Body of Speech Data

Observation has been *the* method used by descriptive linguists. The criteria for observational adequacy may be seen within the techniques of the method, particularly in the procedures used by descriptive linguists – that is, phonetics, phonemics, morphemics, and immediate constituent analysis.

So, descriptive linguistics hoped to see that descriptions of as many instances of speech in all languages of the world be made as possible so that the ways in which languages differ and change might be seen in a comparative way both historically and contemporaneously.

Since the goal involved describing many languages which had no written tradition, linguists found themselves in the position of reducing languages to writing as well. This task facilitated and fostered the spread of literacy. Literacy itself for the descriptive linguist remains a secondary goal; however, in recent decades with the development of sociolinguistics, it is becoming more important in matters of language policy and language planning in developing nations. By understanding the various uses of speech in speech communities through descriptions of actual instances of use in context, sociolinguists may use the data-oriented information gleaned in their forming policy alternatives. Sociolinguists, like descriptive linguists involved in describing language use, find observational criteria the most useful evaluation procedure for their work.

Whereas Bloomfield felt that language change should be understood inductively and that induction (generalizing from a basis of fact) should proceed from observing adequately described data in terms of accounting for the definable entities in a body, Harris's deductive techniques had a different purpose. Championing observational adequacy as the chief evaluation procedure for a grammar, he concurred with Bloomfield that obtaining a "compact one-one representation of the stock of a utterances in the body of speech data is the primary purpose of work in descriptive linguistics. (1951:366) Moreover, since the representation of an utterance or its parts is based on a comparison of utterances, it is really a representation of distinctions. It is this representation of differences which gives us discrete combinatorial elements (each representing a minimal difference). A noncomparative study of speech behavior would probably deal with complex continuous changes, rather than with discrete elements. (1951:367)

As an early structuralist, Harris felt that grammars should be evaluated as observationally adequate, *but* he saw the description of a body of data to be the description based on deduc-

tion rather than on induction.* This difference sparked a debate between linguists favoring IA grammars (observationally
adequate on inductive grounds) and those favoring IP grammars (observationally adequate on deductive grounds). Some
linguists throught an element model "best" described speech
data; others favored a process model.

According to Harris, IP grammar is observationally adequate
if the sequences or elements of speech analyzed are defined
compactly and clearly at each level of description. This grammar differed from that of the Bloomfieldians which itemized
and arranged actual instances of speech. The elements of
speech defined in a Harris grammar were to be more abstract
than the objectively definable and isolatable units which were
to represent all of the distinctions made in a language.

Charles Hockett, a prominent linguist whose work has been
widely read since the 1950s, wisely pointed out that a grammatical description's purpose partially determines its adequacy
although a grammatical description must have a number of
properties to serve any scientific purpose. (1954:229) Essentially, criteria for evaluating grammatical descriptions are the
notions that models of grammatical description such as IA and
IP should:

1. apply to any language;
2. produce results determined by the model and the language
   being analyzed rather than results determined by the
   analyst;

*Deduction and induction refer to two distinct logical processes. "*Deductive*
reasoning is a logical process in which a conclusion drawn from a set of premises contains no more information than the premises taken collectively. *All
dogs are animals; this is a dog; therefore, this is an animal.* The truth of the
conclusion is dependent only on the method. *All men are apes; this is a man;
therefore this is an ape. Inductive* reasoning is a logical process in which a
conclusion is proposed that contains more information than the observations
or experience on which it is based. *Every crow that has ever been seen is
black; therefore, all crows are black.* The truth of the conclusion is verifiable
only in terms of future experience and certainly is attainable only if all possible
instances have been examined. In the example there is no certainty that a
white crow will not be found tomorrow, although past experience would make
such as occurrence seem extremely unlikely." (1969 ed. of *Random House College Dictionary* p. 347)

3. apply to all observed, unobserved, and new data; and
4. contain a "minimum of machinery." (Hockett 1954:229)

Therefore, observationally adequate descriptions of data should be based on a model of grammatical description which is general (applied crosslinguistically), specific (applied to a language particularly), inclusive and predictive, and simple.

These criteria, originally intended as evaluative of descriptions of data from which generalizations might be made about a language, helped to spur the development of IP grammar models. No empirical evidence exists, no matter how complete the language description, that the description of the body of speech data actually accounts for *all* grammatical sentences, *new* sentences, or *only* sentences of that language. IA grammarians hoped that complete descriptions of large enough bodies of data would enable scholars to read the descriptions of the units of speech at the various levels of language in particular languages (items) plus statements of the distribution of those units within the language (arrangements) and thus to analyze newly observed material correctly and predict material not yet encountered.

When some linguists began to think that an account of a body of data could not be evaluated observationally according to such criteria, they chose another goal for their descriptions to achieve, that of DESCRIPTIVE ADEQUACY — the "best" description was that which would give a "correct account of the linguistic intuition of the native speaker." (Chomsky 1964: 923–24) Again we are at the point where linguistics diverged into two streams, one concerned with descriptive adequacy which we are calling linguistics, and the other concerned with observational adequacy which we are calling language description.

Too, with regard to evaluation procedures for the product of linguistic analysis, we see the structuralists in the 1950s again in a "moderate" position as the advocates of IP descriptions of data (predictive) over IA descriptions.

Hockett (1954:230) foresaw the emerging divergence of goals in linguistics, noting that,

> Neither any existing version of IA nor any existing version of
> IP meets all the metacriteria. Insofar as such matters can be felt

quantitatively, it seems to me that IP . . . comes at least as close to satisfying the requirements as IA does, though perhaps no closer. In other words, what we have is two main types of model, neither completely satisfactory. Our course in this case is also clear. We must have more experimentation, as much with one model as with the other — and with the devising of further models too, for that matter — looking towards an eventual reintegration into a single more nearly satisfactory model, but not forcing that reintegration until we are ready for it.

Gleason distinguished a description of data from a description of language. This way, the former covers all the sentences of the data, and only those; the latter covers "many sentences which the linguist had not observed" and constitutes "a prediction of sentences which could reasonably be expected to occur." (1961:197)

Thus, a descriptive grammar may be evaluated as observationally adequate with regard to how well it describes the elements of the language and the processes or arrangements they enter into, given the analytical model of the linguist as applied to the data. A description of observed data should be clear, concise, and observationally adequate.

Explanatory Adequacy

Explanatory adequacy, the ultimate goal of transformational linguists, is reached by applying a theory that "aims to provide a principled basis, independent of any particular language, for the selection of the descriptively adequate grammar of each language." (Chomsky 1964:923–24.) Transformational linguists, remember, are interested in developing a model of the process of language acquisition to portray linguistic competence. But, in their actual work they try to produce descriptively adequate grammars of particular languages, often their own. These linguists use themselves as informants, using their intuition about their native language as means of evaluating the descriptive adequacy of their language description. Thus, they account for what they have never said but could have and what they might some day say, thereby accounting for *all and only* grammatical utterances of their particular language. The resulting account is adequate as long as it describes what native speakers of the language feel to be intuitively correct utterances, as well as actual utterances in their language and accounts.

For descriptive linguists, the *expression* of language is paramount. Descriptive linguistics aims to describe *both* the expression and content of languages as used. The theory and method, however, developed so far for the analysis of content has not kept pace with that of expression. Until both aspects of languages as analyzable data can be uniformly studied and rigorously described, attempting to explain language (as use) or individual languages (as content *and* expression) is pointless. As Gleason (1961:13) aptly noted, "we do not even have a clear idea of the basic unit or units and hence no basis for the high degree of precision which characterizes the study of language expression."

Most linguists agree that the point of linguistics "is to arrive at an understanding of language." (Langacker 1968:16) The descriptivists hope to do this by describing the structure of language as both content and expression. The transformationalists, agreeing with the descriptivists that it is difficult to analyze content in any rigorous procedural way, contend that a different focus might produce an understanding of language. Rather than trying to isolate and analyze distributional elements of content and expression in a body of data, they propose to look at language acquisition since, given that all humans acquire language, an understanding of the process might lead to an understanding of the result—language. How can we relate the goal of understanding language through its acquisition to the criteria of explanatory adequacy which Chomsky cites as a way to evaluate linguistic theory? To clarify this, let us examine some recent claims by Chomsky on this point.

> It is . . . suggested that the language learner (analogously the linguist) approaches the problem of language acquisition (grammar construction) with a schematism that determines in advance the general properties of human language and the general properties of the grammars that may be constructed to account for linguistic phenomena. His task is to select the

highest-valued grammar of the appropriate form compatible with available data. Having done so he knows the language it generates. His knowledge may thus extend far beyond what might be provided by principles of induction, generalization, analogy, substitution, segmentation, and classification of the sort examined in any of the explicit theories of acquisition of language that have been proposed. (1973:12)

Therefore, the linguist *is* the language acquirer and the grammar produced may be evaluated in terms of descriptive adequacy, given the evaluation procedures of the linguistic model being used. In this case, it is a transformational/generative model. The mainstays of the descriptive and structural models include the techniques of induction, generalization, analogy, substitution, segmentation, and classification which Chomsky is suggesting will not allow the linguist to discover the knowledge of language a native speaker has.

Let us see what criteria are proposed to achieve the goal of explanatory adequacy in a description of grammars taken collectively to be a model of the process of language acquisition.

As noted throughout this chapter, attempts to evaluate the results of linguistic analysis of whatever school with whatever goals have given rise to new schools of thought and new models for studying language scientifically. These situations are somewhat analogous to the attempts to evaluate sets of descriptively adequate grammars as explanatorily adequate. Since the criteria of descriptive adequacy itself are rarely met for language specific accounts, how then can criteria for explanatory adequacy be established?

According to Chomsky (1973:14),

Much of the work on linguistic theory since the mid-1950s has been devoted to circumscribing and delimiting the class of potential generative grammars and determining how they function, in an effort to meet this goal and thus to solve the fundamental problem of linguistic theory . . . the problem of characterizing the language faculty and thus accounting for the acquisition of knowledge of language (and, analogously, the problem of justifying the grammars proposed by the linguist for particular languages).

Furthermore, he perceives a difference in depth of explanation of states

> I have suggested in my *Current Issues in Linguistic Theory* [New York: Humanities Press, 1964] that the term "level of descriptive adequacy" might be used for the study of the relation between grammars and data and the term "level of explanatory adequacy" for the relation between a theory of universal grammar and these data. (1972:27 – 28, fn 5)

In fact, transformational/generative grammarians believe they must use available linguistic data to justify empirically the generative grammars they produce. According to Fillmore (1972), the claims made for generative grammars as combining to build a theory of language acquisition are of little value to the linguist dedicated to describing a particular language's structure in the best possible way. But, that linguist is contributing to the available data the theorists may use to justify the descriptive adequacy of their grammars. Ultimately, too, the linguist who describes structure well, in this line of reasoning, contributes to the development of an explanatorily adequate theory of language.

To Fillmore, articulated, well-defined goals of evaluating a formalization of the language-acquisition process, such as those of descriptive and explanatory adequacy, are artifacts of the theoretical linguists and valid for their purposes. Fillmore calls the modern descriptive/structural linguist a "new taxonomist." Included in this category are the linguists who describe data in an effort to include the structure of both the content and expression sides of spoken language. They are using some of the newer ideas of the structural linguistics which gave rise to PS grammar and also of tagmemics and stratificational grammar (models of description which will be discussed in the next chapter). According to Fillmore (1972:18), the new taxonomist "will be glad if he can be reassured that his success as a grammarian will not be measured on the basis of his ability to demonstrate that his grammar does everything that generative grammars have been said to have to do. I believe he deserves such reassurance." Moreover, "if he is a practitioner of the New Taxonomy, he is having a good time. It is possible to remain happy, for a while, without well-defined goals."

The transformationalist/generativists, unlike the new taxonomists, after the period dominated by Chomsky's *Syntactic Structures* approach (1957) have stopped producing grammars. Many linguists feel that assuming generative grammars for human languages could be constructed showed naïveté. So, linguistics, unlike language description today, is no longer aimed primarily at producing grammars. Actually,

> if the pursuit of generative grammars has not led to the construction of viable generative grammars, it has led to a deepening appreciation of just what a fantastic system each human has articulated within him. The pursuit of a precise formulation of grammar, although it has not brought precise formulations which are valid, has created a correct attitude, an attitude which previous work did not engender. (Postal 1972:161.

Yet the new taxonomists are attempting to produce grammars rather than explain the nature of language. Postal criticizes linguists who know and document a welter of facts but never realize that their facts only reflect some underlying mystery whose nature they hardly fathom. (ibid.)

In Postal's terms, the fact-conscious linguists were not attempting to touch the essential nature of language's mystery but rather were and are trying to analyze and describe actual instances of utterances. So, observational adequacy is a goal to be achieved provided "the grammar presents the observed primary data correctly." (Chomsky 1966:28) We have seen that the goal is more closely achieved in the description of expression in language. We will see further that efforts are underway to present the data from the content side of language correctly as well. Explanatory adequacy, then, is a goal of linguistic theory. The clearest statement of the goal as a solution to the task of linguistics as opposed to the task of language description is the following by Chomsky (1972:67):

> The fundamental problem of linguistic theory . . . is to account for the choice of particular grammar, given the data available to the language learner. To account for this inductive leap, linguistic theory must try to characterize a fairly narrow class of grammars that are available to the language learner; it must, in other words, specify the notion "human lan-

guage" in a narrow and restrictive fashion. A "better theory," then, is one that specifies the class of possible grammars so narrowly that some procedure of choice or evaluation can select a descriptively adequate grammar for each language from this class, within reasonable conditions of time and access to data. Given alternative linguistic theories that meet this condition, we might compare them in terms of general "simplicity" or other metatheoretic notions, but it is unlikely that such considerations will have any more significance within linguistics than they do in any other field. For the moment, the problem is to construct a general theory of language that is so richly structured and so restrictive in the conditions it imposes that, while meeting the condition of descriptive adequacy, it can sufficiently narrow the class of possible grammars so that the problem of choice of grammar (and explanation in some serious sense) can be approached.

Summary

Adequacy of both linguistic and language description may be considered to be of three general types: observational, descriptive, explanatory. Each type is measurable by a set of criteria determined largely by the goals of the description under consideration. Descriptions purporting to record and analyze representative samples of speech in a body of data are best judged by how well the descriptions achieve their respective goals. If the description allows for someone reading it to reproduce the body of data in such a way that it can be repeated, then the task of descriptive linguistics has been achieved. Such a description is observationally adequate because it lets us observe what a native speaker said. Confronted with another description of the same data, the criteria for determining observational adequacy allows us to choose the most compact description as the most adequate. Linguists differed as to whether or not observational adequacy should best be judged inductively or deductively. However if the linguist's description purports to describe *la langue* rather than *la parole*, then observational adequacy (particularly judged on inductive grounds) becomes pointless. Observational adequacy is not useful here because *la langue* is not observable but rather

> . . . is a storehouse filled by the numbers of a given community through their active use of speaking, a grammatical system that has a potential existence in each brain, or, more specifically, in the brains of a group of individuals. For language [as *langue*] is not complete in any speaker; it exists perfectly only within a collectivity. (DeSaussure 1966:13)

It makes little sense to judge a description of the storehouse of a potential grammatical system in terms of observational adequacy. *Langue* is not describable by presenting an analyzed record of the speech of an individual speaker. A language description is adequate to the extent that it portrays the shared grammatical system of a speech community. Strictly speaking, criteria for determining what constitutes an adequate description of langue are difficult to make explicit since language is a nonobjective conceptual entity that is verifiable. The criteria of descriptive adequacy do not strictly apply because they center on whether or not the description at issue accurately reflects the linguistic intuition of a native speaker of any language. A language description also seeks to account for the common system of relationships speakers of a particular language share. However, to the extent that it describes linguistic knowledge, criteria of descriptive adequacy applied to structural analyses make no sense. They are relevant as long as they are applied to evaluate structural analyses.

Within each school of linguists there developed principles of measurement to be applied to the analytical product. Although neither descriptive nor observational adequacy seemed applicable to structural descriptions of language, various structuralist camps (American, Czech, French, Danish) established their own criteria. The glossematic school particularly exemplified this phenomenon.

The glossematicians introduced the idea that adequacy, as measured by how well an analysis depicted the language system, ought to be determined by internal criteria. That is, all structural analyses ought to be measurable by a set of structuralist adequacy criteria. The corollary of this is that the descriptivist, transformationalist schools should do likewise. Meanwhile, external adequacy criteria could be applied to the field of language science, given its stated general goals.

Next came the notion of metalanguage. The evaluation of competing structural analyses in part involved comparing the languages used for the description of language by the various schools. If two structural analyses of the same language accounted for the same relationships yet used differently labeled and constructed structural units, they could be judged equally adequate as descriptive accounts of the particular linguistic system. Such analyses are notational variants of each other. Eventually, it would be desirable to unify the descriptive units used so that each account of *langue* would use a common metalanguage. The chief criterion for evaluating competing structural analyses of *la langue* amounted to comparing notationally variant analyses in such a way that the best analysis satisfied the structuralist notion of simplicity.

Simplicity as a measure of the adequacy of a linguistic description would "liberate" structural linguists from the bounds of evaluating their analyses using observational adequacy. Simplicity freed linguists from the insistence imposed by observational criteria that every description must contain the levels of every other one and that each description should essentially re-record data.

In fact, linguists realized that linguistic descriptions ought to be evaluated both internally and externally and that evaluative criteria ought to be kept separate.

Explanatory adequacy as a goal to be met by descriptions of linguistic material is a goal established specifically for evaluating entire theories of language to the extent that one theory accounts for descriptively adequate grammars of particular languages to a greater extent than another theory. Thus, explanatory adequacy becomes a realistic goal only for descriptions of linguistic intuition.

The criteria for evaluating descriptions of actual language use and for evaluating descriptions of proposed models of linguistic theory rest on notions of what constitutes an adequate description. Linguistic theory seeks to achieve explanatory adequacy. Actual descriptions of language data seek to achieve observational adequacy. Descriptive adequacy is the goal of descriptions characterizing the linguistic intuitions of native speakers of particular languages. Each goal is valid and has measurable ways to determine whether one description as compared to another comes closer to achieving it.

For Thought and Discussion

1. Describe briefly the three adequacies. Is there a hierarchial arrangement in your opinion? Are they mutually exclusive or inclusive?
2. Each of the language theories described has a formalized method of interpreting data. Do they all look at the same data? Why might a transformationalist be confined to looking only at his/her native language?
3. What is a metalanguage? Give some of its main elements for each of the three schools of linguistics discussed.
4. In your opinion, is it valid to evaluate structuralism and transformational grammar by comparing them? What about structuralism and descriptive linguistics? Or descriptive linguistics and transformational grammar?
5. What is the simplicity criterion? How does it differ from the principle of the three adequacies as a measure for evaluation of grammars?
6. What is the difference in approach to observational adequacy between descriptive linguistics and structuralism? Using Hockett's evaluation measures, how would you evaluate each?
7. What does the model of transformational grammar approximate? Why are descriptive and structural grammars inadequate for achieving these goals?
8. Is there an evaluation of linguistic goals inherent in the principle of the three adequacies? In your opinion, are the goals of one of the theories discussed more valid than those of another?

ᐦFOUR

ᐊltenative ᗰethods and Techniques of ᒪanguage Description

Up to now we have examined the descriptivist, structuralist, and early transformationalist schools, noting that, as the approaches to the study of language differed in their targets of analysis, so did the criteria for evaluating them and the results.

We will now consider other current positions in the study of linguistic theory and language description—specifically tagmemics, computational linguistics (machine translation), stratificational grammar, and componential analysis—as well as the uses to which these various approaches have been put.

Tagmemics

TAGMEMICS, a behaviorist approach to language in its theoretical stance, is diametrically opposed to the rationalist transformationalist theoretical view. Tagmemics emerged at the same time that Chomsky introduced and began to develop his theory of transformational grammar. However, the origins of the tagmemic approach can be traced to Bloomfield's mechanistic view of language (1933) and to Kenneth Pike's earlier works (1943, 1947). For example, Pike regarded tagmemics as just one part of a "unified theory of the structure of human behavior." (1954, 1967)

BEHAVIORISM is a theory which holds that observation is the only valid data for describing knowledge. Conversely, RATIONALISM is a theory which holds that reason or intellect, rather than observed behavior, is the actual source of knowledge.

Tagmemics, evolved from descriptive linguistics, is strongly behavioristic. As such, its theory and method are heavily empirical. Empiricism, as opposed to rationalism, is a theory which holds that experience from the senses is the only source of knowledge. Conversely, transformational grammar is primarily rationalistic. Tagmemics seeks to describe the content and expression of speech as language behavior. Transformational grammar seeks to characterize the nature of human language (competence and performance) as linguistic knowledge. Thus, the two approaches to language have different origins and vastly different goals. Langacker (1968:235) expressed the empiricist and rationalist traditions in linguistics this way:

> At one extreme, it could be claimed that no linguistic structure is innately specified, that language is learned entirely through experience. This is the empiricist view . . . It holds that we have no special, inborn capacity to acquire language. The fact that we acquire language and the structure of the language we learn are both due to the training we receive as children . . . At the opposite extreme, we find the rationalist view that language is innately specified almost in its entirety. Children learn to talk because the capacity for language, as well as most of the structure of language, is built into them.

With the particular view of language as behavior, tagmemicists, in stressing the importance of data gathering, believe that theories must be grounded in facts and that "somebody has to paddle in the empirical mud to find them." (Algeo 1974:1)

Assertions Made by Tagmemics

As a model of grammatical description, tagmemics makes "assertions about the characteristics of rational human communication." (Hale 1974, fn 1:55) As such, it embodies a number of ideas about behavior along with specific procedures for linguists to use to examine their data.

The notions ETIC and EMIC, as first put forth by Pike for phonetics and phonemics, are central to tagmemic analysis at all levels of the description of the hierarchical structure of language. Throughout tagmemic analysis, whether of all behavior or mainly linguistic behavior, an etic view is one consisting of observations outside the system. In phonetics, the initial data transcribed is outside the system. The procedure of phonemic analysis refines these initial data to reveal what is important to speakers of the language being analyzed. The mass of initial observations of behavior are etic while the emic view is "concerned with the contrastive, patterned system of a specific language or culture or universe of discourse, with the way a participant in a system sees the system, as well as with distinctions between contrastive units." (Waterhouse 1974:6)

In tagmemic analysis the phoneme is the basic unit of the phonological hierarchy. As opposed to descriptive linguistics, tagmemics posits a parallel basic unit for the grammatical hierarchy—the tagmeme. A TAGMEME is a syntactic unit and is identifiable as the correlation of a slot with its filler. A SLOT is a "specific grammatical function" and its FILLER is "the class of items which performs that function" (Waterhouse 1974:6), that is, the filler is what fills the slot.

Tagmemes are written as formulas. For example, +S:NP is a tagmeme. The + indicates that the particular sentence (clause, phrase, and so on) being analyzed requires a subject slot to occur. The slot referred to in the formula is S (subject). The colon in the formula means "manifested by." (Longacre 1964:24) The NP (noun phrase) is the filler; +S:NP is a syntactic unit (tagmeme) stating that, in the unit being analyzed, there is a required subject slot and the one occurring in this instance is filled by a noun phrase. Thus, one reads +S:NP as "the obligatory subject slot is manifested by a noun phrase."

In the tagmemic framework, language is viewed as structure. The concept of structure, however, differs somewhat from what we have encountered before in these pages. In tagmemics structure is hierarchical so that, in a language, units may be identified at different levels. This is the view prevalent in descriptive linguistics. We saw in Chapter One that morphemes occur at a higher level of analysis than phonemes and yet are composed of phonemes. In the tagmemic approach to language, structure is not composed of separate levels; instead "there are three simultaneous hierarchies . . . : lexicon, phonology, and grammar." (Waterhouse 1974:5) Each hierarchy is composed of small units which are combined into larger units. The small units are composed of still smaller units.

A basic assumption of tagmemics is that there are three "semi-autonomous but interlocking modes — phonology, grammar, and lexicon." (Longacre 1974:11) Within each mode there are levels of units which are describable. For example, in the phonological hierarchy above the phoneme are "higher-level-phonological units such as syllables and stress groups." Likewise in both the grammar and lexicon, units are viewed as multileveled.

As a hierarchical structure in its own right, the lexicon is a defining feature of tagmemics. This "new lexemic hierarchy has been set up with the lexeme as its basic unit." (Waterhouse 1974:13) In the tagmemic view, the lexicon represents a third component of linguistic structure entirely separate from phonology and grammar.

A tagmemic description of language consists of describing the phonology, grammar and lexicon at each level within each hierarchy. These are described "in terms of the contrasts between them, of the variants each has, and of their distribution in larger units and as members of classes and systems of units." (*ibid.*) Basically, tagmemics extends the procedures of descriptive linguistics above the morphemic level in a consistent way. Since what tagmemicists call grammar includes both morphology and now also syntax as described by its basic unit, they have abandoned the descriptivist doctrine that levels of grammatical description must not be mixed.

Where the descriptivist analyzes phonology without reference to grammar and meaning, the tagmemicist holds that, in language learning in a field situation, grammatical patterns, meaningful units, and correct pronunciation of sounds must be mastered simultaneously. Since this is how languages are learned, tagmemicists reason, why should not hierarchies be analyzed simultaneously? Within the hierarchy of grammar, tagmemes as basic units combine into larger units called SYN-TAGMEMES. Just as in descriptive linguistics, phonemic analysis involves displaying the results in a form of notation produced by the method (for example, slashes to enclose phonemes, square brackets for allophones, and so on), in tagmemic analysis the results, too, are displayed notationally. For example, consider an analysis of the sentence *The boy has the book* i.e., +S:NP + T Pred:TVP + O:NP. The analysis is read as follows:

> obligatory subject slot filled by noun phrase, followed by transitive predicate slot filled by obligatory transitive verb phrase, followed by obligatory object slot filled by noun phrase. (Waterhouse 1974:11)

In other words, the sentence is a syntagmeme composed of three tagmemes: +S:NP, +T Pred:TVP, +O:NP. The + means the tagmeme is obligatory in the construction; correspondingly, the − would mean it is optional.

The hierarchies of language—lexicon, phonology, and grammar—have distinct types of hierarchical structuring to be described in a tagmemic analysis. For phonology, sounds are described in the MANIFESTATION MODE as they occur as phonemes with allophonic distribution. For grammar, filled slots are described in the DISTRIBUTION MODE as tagmemes with morphemes as a basic unit. For the lexicon, lexical items are described in the FEATURE MODE with lexemes as the basic unit. (Waterhouse 1974:12–13)

In the manifestation mode, what is stated is the set of actual and potential variants a unit has. Consider the following examples to illustrate the manifestation mode of tagmemic analysis:

> . . . for instance, the command *You come here!* can take three forms: *You come here; Come here; Come here, you.* These are the etic manifestations of the sentence, its description in the "manifestation mode." . . . In baseball, for exam-

ple, "striking a foul ball" has two features: hitting the ball and failing to drive it in a line between third and first base. But it has numerous manifestations, including merely ticking the ball, driving it straight up in the air, or driving it to the left of third or to the right of first. The emic description tells *what* a foul ball is; the etic description tells the *ways* it can happen. (Bolinger 1975:524)

The ways it happens are its manifestations. Allophones are manifestations of phonemes, allomorphs are manifestations of morphemes. To the tagmemicist, the manifestation mode is also known as VARIATION STRUCTURE. Each hierarchy may be analyzed in terms of the variation structure of the units within it.

Yet the feature mode involves identifying units as they occur in contrast with other units. This is done by comparing the occurrence of a unit with the occurrence of other units in various contexts. The idea in the feature mode is that this comparison of contexts of occurrence allows the analysis to get at meaning in an objective way. Contrasting contexts of occurrence for units being described show in what *situational roles* the units may occur. For example, subjects may have a number of roles determinable by the contexts in which the noun phrases used as subjects occur. Some subjects may be actual instruments of an action, or of goals, locations, and so on. Sentences are described in the feature mode with respect to what the subject and predicate specifically are in terms of their function. For example, the actual forms used, along with what functions the forms filling the various slots have in a sentence, are stated. Tagmemicists consider the situational roles played by NPs to be behavioral features. To them meaning is analyzed by stating contrasting contexts of occurrences of units with contrasting functions. The functions are situational roles which are relatable to grammatical roles such as subject and object. When stated, the relationship of situational and grammatical roles is a behavioral objective description of meaning-in a structural sense.

Thus, the feature mode is unlike any mode or type of grammatical analysis discussed thus far. Where we have been able to exemplify the manifestation mode through parallels with phonetics and phonemics, describing what the feature mode refers to is not as easy. Tagmemicists refer to the feature mode of language as its CONTRAST STRUCTURE.* According to Pike (1954:36),

> The *feature mode* of an emic unit of activity will in general be viewed as comprised of simultaneously occurring identificational-contrastive components, with its internal segmentation analyzed with special reference to stimulus-response features (including purpose or lexical meaning, where relevant).

Meaning, in tagmemics, is a type of awareness of purpose which, like the grammatical and phonological levels of language's hierarchies, can be analyzed through the use of mechanical procedures.

Given the behavioristic orientation of tagmemics, we now turn to the tagmemicist view of what underlies linguistic behavior. Pike and the tagmemicists apply the word HYPOSTASIS to the underlying nature of the units of linguistic behavior. Within the feature mode, what is called a conceptualized hypostasis is beneath-surface meaning. But, according to the tagmemicist, the linguist needs a technique for studying the concepts that underlie a speaker's awareness of meaning "as a specialized instance of a broader technical principal of responses elicited in context." (Pike 1954:79) Thus, meaning in the tagmemicist sense is, through its stimulus-response orientation, a characteristically behavioristic view. In addition to tagmemic analysis as outlined so far, tagmemics as a type of grammatical description uses what is called matrix analysis in displaying data. In tagmemics, the linguistic matrix is "a table of language elements: rows and columns represent significant properties of a structural system or subsystem; entries in the boxes of the table signal properties of the system; and— preferably—the rows and columns are ordered so as to show in the most effective way possible the relation of the semantic properties of the system to groups of entries in the table." (Pike 1970:ix)

---

*In the summary at the end of this chapter we will look briefly at case grammar which arose out of TG grammar in an effort to deal with meaning. Interestingly enough, case grammar shows a number of parallels with the feature mode of tagmemic analysis.

For example, clause types and sentence types in a language may be displayed on a matrix. Robert Longacre (1964) performed a tagmemic analysis of the Zoque language spoken west of the Mayan area in southern Mexico. In that analysis he categorized clause types as follows:

	ORDERS	INDICATIVE	SUBORDINATE	INTERROGATIVE	IMPERATIVE
	Intransitive	X	X	X	X
TYPES	Transitive	X	X	X	X
	Ditransitive	X	X	X	X
	Descriptive	X	X	X	

After Longacre 1964:60

Clause types, sentence types, and other classes of units of analysis are placed on matrices based on dimensions of contrast and similarity. The four-by-four matrix of Zoque clause types accounts for the fifteen clause types encountered in Zoque data. The matrix indicates that there are four clause types and four clause orders in Zoque. It also indicates that among the descriptive type clauses, there are no occurrences of an imperative order (mood). Within each order—indicative, subordinate, interrogative, imperative—the clause types have different characteristics. Each clause type may occur in any of the orders except that descriptive clauses do not occur as imperatives in Zoque.

Other matrices are used in the analysis of the language (here in its distribution structure) to show that there are subtypes of each clause order. For example, according to Longacre, in Zoque there are six kinds of subordinate clauses: manner, location, time, cause, purpose, participial. Each kind of subordinate clause may further be analyzed as a transitive, intrasitive, ditransitive, or descriptive type.

When a matrix is established at any level of analysis by the tagmemicist, the next task is to confirm the analysis and seek clues as to likely fillers for empty boxes on the matrix. Of the Zoque clause analysis done on a matrix, Longacre (1964:61) holds that it "seems to confirm the types posited—some of which were found after a preliminary matrix of the same general shape was found to contain lacunae. The nonoccurrence of descriptive imperative remains, however, as a genuine lacuna."

The matrix in tagmemic analysis is designed to show relations "between constructions in general (not merely between sentences) by conceptualizing them as chartered together in various dimensions." (Longacre 1964:16) In the matrix just examined we looked at the various clause types and orders in Zoque. Clauses are just one level of the Zoque grammatical hierarchical system. Other levels of the grammatical hierarchy amenable to matrix analysis are stem, word, phrase, sentence, and so on. Further, the levels of the phonological and lexical hierarchies are analyzable on matrices as well, in terms of the contrasts, similarities, and variations exhibited by their units. At this point in the discussion of tagmemics, it would be desirable to give an example of a tagmemic analysis of a particular body of data. In comparison with other models of grammatical description, however, the form of a grammar has been discussed only rarely in the literature. In fact, to be a tagmemicist one need not subscribe to any particular doctrine dictating the form or notation system a grammar should use. Unlike other models of grammatical description, tagmemics has no particular formalism or set of rule types or schema for a grammar complete with specifications of components and their input-output relationships. (ibid., note 1:55)

In his *Grammar Discovery Procedures*, a field manual for conducting tagmemic analysis, Longacre (1964:8) instructs the reader that "to describe a language exhaustively (a task as yet seriously attempted by no one), three volumes are needed: a phonological statement, a grammatical statement, and a highly sophisticated dictionary." He goes on to stress that tagmemic procedures develop three methods of analysis and each approach is distinct from the other, yet

> Grammatical analysis leads to formulae, statements, and operations which can generate the grammatical patterns of novel utterances beyond the scope of one's corpus. But, until joined to a full set of phonological rules . . . and to a complete cross-reference dictionary, the grammatical specifications cannot generate actual utterances. (1964:9)

In general, a tagmemic grammar is envisioned as a series of tagmemic formulas which give "map-like summaries of constructions." Descriptions of entire sentences as utterances can only be made with information from the three hierarchies stated together. Thus, an utterance would be described in three statements: one of its variation structure through an analysis of the variants units have in each hierarchy, one of its contrast structure through analysis of the situational roles lexical units have, and one of its distribution structure through elaborations of tagmemic formulas and matrix analysis.

Tagmemicists believe that the analysis of actual utterances gathered from informants is what is important, holding that this analysis is best accomplished by using the three methods of analysis for a language's three hierarchical structures. The three methods of analysis stem from the approaches taken to each hierarchy and may be seen as analogous to the notions of *particle, wave* and *field.* These ideas figure in the theory behind tagmemics as a behaviorist approach to language description.

The concepts of particle, wave, and field provide what Pike holds to be a multiple viewpoint from which human behavior (including language) may be profitably examined. As we have already indicated, each hierarchy of language is described in a particular mode. That is, the phonology is described in the manifestation mode, the lexicon is described in the feature mode, and the grammar is described in the distribution mode. Each mode has its own characteristic basic unit. Pike contends further that the basic unit of each mode reflects one of the structure concepts. The manifestation mode reflects its basic unit "as a continuous wave of activity without discrete boundaries." The feature mode reflects its basic unit "as a discrete particle with its own identity and contrasting with all other discrete particles—phonemes, morphemes, or tagmemes." The distribution mode reflects its unit "as a position in a field or a cell on a matrix." (Algeo 1974:5)

To illustrate this, Algeo claims that by conceiving the units of each hierarchical structure thusly: "A phoneme can be located in the traditional articulation chart" representing *wave* or continuous activity through the *manifestation mode (variation* structure). Morphemes can be conceived of on a graph or continuum (for example, as "measured by a semantic differential scale") representing *particle* or discrete contrasting identity through the *feature mode (contrast* structure).

Tagmemes can be considered as if they occur in a *field* of relational grammatical characteristics shown by their position on a matrix through the *distribution mode* (*distribution* structure).

Referring to this theoretical viewpoint of Pike as the PRINCIPLE OF TRIMODALITY, Algeo holds that it has ramifications for a theoretical approach to all behavior. In other words:

> Everything can be seen as consisting of contrastive features, with variant manifestations and distributional relations. Lexicon, phonology, and grammar analogize not only with particle, wave, and field; but also with segment, hierarchy, and matrix; with item, process, and relation; with point, line, and space; with science, art, and philosophy; and even with the true, the beautiful, and the good. *We tremble on the verge of a Father-feature, Son-manifestation, and Holy Ghost-distribution that would make proto-tagmemicists out of the conciliar fathers of Nicaea* (italics mine). (Algeo 1974:5 – 6)

Pike (1974:5–6) sees the three perspectives of particle, wave, and field as representative of differences and changes in the observer's stance "which allows representation of the same materials either as a set of particles (with variants), or as a set of waves, or as a point or points in a set of intersecting features (as a field).

Machine Translation

We have seen that descriptive linguistics and tagmemics are models of grammatical description which deal with developing mechanical techniques for segmenting speech data into units at various levels of analysis. In the mid-1950s, many linguists became interested in using machines for the objective analysis of language as accumulated speech data.

The general field in which computers are used by linguists is known as COMPUTATIONAL LINGUISTICS. It covers automatic syntactic analysis, sentence generation, grammar testing, concordance construction, automatic abstracting, information retrieval, stylistic studies, content processing, semantic classification studies and other forms of text analysis. Linguists concerned with the actual use of language by a speaker or listener also use computers when investigating speech production and recognition.

As noted in Chapter Two and as will be seen again in Chapter Five, computers have played a part in the development of both PS grammar and TG grammar. Moreover, machines can be used to generate sentences by applying rules to strings of morphemes. As seen in the definition above, computational linguistics, like linguistics, has two basic tasks: linguistic theory and language description.

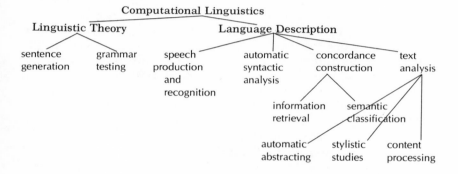

Moreover, as Garvin (1963:4) observed, they are "interrelated in that the concepts of linguistic theory can be used as points of departure for the methodological devices of linguistic description." Unlike tagmemicists, computational linguists date the origins of their theoretical underpinnings to the trend away from behavioral psychology toward mathematics and symbolic logic. While tagmemicists advanced the ideas for describing the hierarchical structure of speech begun by the Bloomfieldian descriptivists, computational linguists such as Chomsky and his followers in their early work heeded Harris's call to formalize the structure of the system of language. While Chomsky's work led to theoretical linguistics, one aspect of computational linguistics (that for which we are using the cover term machine translation) aimed at language description.

The Machine Translation Period and Language Description

Chomsky's ideas were influenced somewhat by a mathematical theory of communication developed by Shannon and Weaver. Shannon and Weaver were also influential in the rise of the machine translation (henceforth, MT). To Weaver, it appeared the computer's logical circuits could analyze the language's logical elements. Shannon's ideas about information theory could suggest means to begin the analysis of meaning as conveyed in translation. Shannon and Weaver saw that ultimately machine research on language would have to deal with "the common base of human communication—the real but as yet undiscovered universal language." (Delavenay 1960:29)

Linguists and electronics engineers worked jointly, aiming to study the "word frequency and language-to-language equivalence" in scientific texts, develop methods for using electronic memories and producing automatic dictionaries, and carry out syntactic analyses which would make it possible for computer programs to translate a text from one language to another.

MT was posited on the idea that automatic dictionaries to effect word-for-word translation would be the best approach. This goal was expanded to that of producing an automatic and grammatically correct translation of one language to another.

Interestingly enough, MT was in part politically inspired. Americans and Russians dominated the resultant research; the former aimed to translate Russian into English, and the latter vice versa. In 1946, Weaver suggested that decoding methods used during World War II might be useful in analyzing languages. A. D. Booth, an Englishman, added the idea of storing "word-for-word" equivalents (such as occur in a dictionary) in an electronic computer. Therefore, a record of decoded equivalents could be kept for use in translation of large bodies of material. Both Americans and Russians began to

> base their work on the idea that the special requirements of the treatment of linguistic data by computers provide an instrument for linguistic analysis which enriches our knowledge of language, an instrument capable of exploring the differ-

ences existing between systems of expression of two languages. (Delavenay 1960:41)

In MT, too, we note again, that, as with each "new" model of grammatical description, it begins at the level which brought problems to previous models. In MT the target was primarily the development of an automatic dictionary of forms to be matched with content equivalents in another language.

To translate from Language B is to attempt to reconstitute, with the system of expression of Language B, the meaning of a sentence or string of sentences, expressed in Language A by means of the system of expression peculiar to that language. The meaning of a sentence is the representation in the speaker's mind, materialized by means of phonetic and visual symbols grouped into words. Each word possesses, or may possess, several values, semantic or grammatical. Each word may be syntactically associated with other words in a number of ways. Perception of meaning is dependent on the determination of these different values and associations. Translation becomes possible only after an analysis of all the linguistic elements of language A, or source language, constituting meaning, embodied in the words and in the relations between words, i.e., semantic values, grammatical values (whether expressed by inflexions or otherwise) and syntactic values. This analysis is followed by a synthesis of the linguistic elements of Language B, or target language, selected because they make it possible to render approximately the same meaning as the original sentence in Language A, and combined according to the rules peculiar to Language B. (Delavenay 1960:45)

From this we can see that MT efforts hoped to provide a means of linking the content and expression sides of language, thereby overcoming one of the stumbling blocks of descriptive linguistics. The main operations of MT are the analysis of the source language and a synthesis of the target language.

In general, MT involves three phases: analysis of the input sentence, conversion of one source to another target, and decoding of the converted code to an output sentence or text.

Attempts to accomplish MT revealed a number of problems. Primarily, the analyzed parts converted to the synthesized whole did not necessarily jibe. What happens to inflected endings in one language which do not occur in the other? What are the grammatical values of uninflected words? What is done with words having a number of meanings? In 1960 the future of MT seemed bright. As one linguist summarized the state of the art at that time:

> An attempt has been made to explore the complexity of linguistic data, and it has already been established, for example, that the translation of a twenty-word sentence may require as many as 10,000 logical machine operations. If the translation of more complex sentences is to be performed rapidly enough to be economically interesting, we shall have to discover more expeditious methods making it possible to reduce such operations to a minimum and economize some millionths of a second per word. The exploration of linguistic structures will have to be pursued to the very end, so that we may discover whether it is really possible to translate not word-by-word but clause-by-clause, as anticipated by the structuralists. We shall have to solve the problems of self-programming so that the machine can choose for itself the most effective programme for a given structure. (Delavenay 1960:116)

In 1976, Rudolph C. Troike, as director of the Center for Applied Linguistics, commented on the present state and future of MT. Alluding to "a widespread myth among linguists that machine translation, or properly machine-aided translation . . . was found to be a failure and has since been abandoned," he argued that the myth is false and urged that new efforts in MT be undertaken. Actually, however, since the early 1960s much research has been curtailed. In the late 1950s and early 1960s, much time, effort and funding was put into developing computer programs for translation. Of these only one became operational: the one at Georgetown University on which two current programs at Oak Ridge and Wright-Patterson Air Force Base are based. Troike believes that the Georgetown program as a research base must be updated if progress is to be made in MT again.

In 1966 the Automatic Language Processing Advisory

Committee (ALPAC) reported that the promise of MT research in the 1950s had not been realized. Consequently, from 1966 to the present, support for MT research has been drastically curtailed. Troike argues that, considering advances in both computer technology and linguistics since 1966, it would be fruitful to encourage MT research again so that it would "not only improve the quality and efficiency of translation, but would add to our knowledge of substantive universals and semantics, as well as deepen our understanding of particular languages."

It would seem that, as a model of language description, MT, with its necessary focus on content and capacity for handling vast amounts of data, would benefit from renewed research. MT attempts to provide a set of discovery procedures for recognizing the content of a document in order to translate it into another language.

> Prior to machine translation, descriptive linguists were mostly concerned with the formal features of language and considered linguistic meaning only to the extent to which it has bearing on formal distinctions. In translation on the other hand — both human and machine translation — meaning becomes the primary subject of interest. Relations between forms are no longer dealt with for their own sake; they are now treated in terms of the function they have as carriers of meaning. Meaning is granted an independent theoretical existence of a sort, since it is only by assuming a content as separate from the form of a particular language that one can decide whether a passage in one language is indeed the translation of a passage in another language: they are if they both express the same, or at least roughly the same, content; they are not if they do not. (Garvin 1963:119)

In traditional descriptive and structural linguistics, informants are considered the primary source of data, and text is seen as an alternative source. In MT, "data collected by textual research have a certain validity that data obtained from informants can never possess." (Hays 1963:186) Implicit in this assertion is the belief that it is practically impossible to elicit data from enough informants to be certain to get every particular of a language, especially things informants have never seen or heard. Therefore, one of the innovations of machine translation as a model of grammatical description is its focus away from informants to text-based methods of data collection.

The description of a grammar of a language based on the analysis of textual materials necessarily requires a very large body of data. Automatic digital computers were hailed when they were developed because they made it possible to handle vast quantities of data economically.

As we saw with descriptive linguistics, it was originally thought that grammatical analysis should proceed from lower to higher levels. In MT the type of grammatical analysis known as automatic analysis was conceived of in the same way.

> An automatic system for grammatical analysis is usually conceived as working its way upward from level to level. First morphological analysis is carried out in accordance with morphological criteria (and lower-level criteria as well; similarity of sound or spelling is used in deciding whether two forms are forms of the same word). Next syntactic analysis is carried out, using morphological and syntactic criteria. Then semantic analysis, using semantic and syntactic criteria, is performed. How far the sequence of levels continues is still an open question, but the proposed automatic analysis programs pass from level to level in one direction only. (Hays 1963: 212–13)

David Hays, a computational linguist, saw, as Pike did in his work with tagmemics, that analysis from lower to higher levels appeared to operate in exactly the opposite fashion as actual informants operated. Moreover, informants employed all levels of language simultaneously. Hays (1963:213) concluded that perhaps the best program for MT would be one that could analyze data going forward and then backward. This move away from the strict separation of levels of grammatical description seems to be common among the new models of grammatical description proposed since early descriptive linguistics.

Linguists involved in executing translations from one language to another with machines realize that they must keep abreast not only of developments in linguistic analytical methods, but of the idea that linguistic theory, in trying to locate linguistic universals through understanding language and the acquisition process, will lead to an integration of theory and method. This will make their endeavors at translation more likely to succeed. In fact, some computational linguists work in automated language acquisition (learning) with this goal in mind.

Fromkin and Rodman (1974) explain that the idea for MT originally was that computers might be used instead of humans as translators but that certain problems resulted because computers are not human! Many computational linguists first thought that a program could be written so that the multitudinous morphemes of one language could be stored in the computer's memory. Then, a dictionary or list of corresponding morphemes in another language could be matched to those of the first language using a program that could add, substitute, delete, and rearrange morphemes.

Fromkin and Rodman (1974:330) offer an interesting example in which the "simple" substitution of one morpheme for another could lead to great difficulties. They cite a Russian computer trying to translate an English text in which the word *light* occurs. This single word in English can mean many things in different functional contexts, for example,

> *the light flooded the room*   N
> *a light car is economical*   ADJ
> *arsonists light fires for fun*   V

and can function in many ways. Each possible use of the one English word *light* would correspond to a different Russian word.

Lack of functions to interpret morphemes in context both syntactically and semantically made the results of early morpheme-to-morpheme translations relatively unsuccessful.

Until linguistic theory and method can account for and analyze syntax and semantics, MT will be equally limited. However, computers can be and are being used by linguists to dissolve semantic ambiguities and perform complex translational syntactic operations. Computers can do rough translations from a source to a target language, provided the linguist can select the correct translation from all the possible ones produced by a computer. As syntactic and semantic analysis becomes more developed in the various approaches to language description and as language theory in general becomes more explicit, the more hope there is for automatic analysis and successful MT.

Stratificational Grammar

Another type of grammatical description, stratificational grammar, provides a direct link with the previously discussed models of descriptive, tagmemic and automatic grammatical analysis. The link, of course, is in the idea of STRATA or levels of description.

Sydney Lamb is the linguist most known for the development of stratificational grammar. We closed the previous section on MT by saying that that field awaits further work on linguistic descriptions of syntax and semantics. It was just this need that spurred Lamb on.

Some linguists label Lamb a descriptivist *à la* Pike and Gleason, yet like the European and American structuralists (Hjelmslev and Harris), he concerned himself with language as a system of relationships rather than as a series of separate hierarchical levels composed of isolatable units. To him, a totality consisted of relationships, not things. Like the formal structuralists, he felt that language is best described in terms of its processes and that these involve the whole system of language at once, rather than processes at one level and then another.

The stratificationalist idea that language, as encoded and decoded communicative behavior, is a unitary process caused stratificational grammarians to spurn models of grammatical description which described processes at separate levels, adopting instead a holistic view of the communicational process. It perhaps appears ironic that a model of grammatical description centering on levels would agree with other postdescriptivist models that levels should not be kept separate.

Regarding the now-familiar debate among competing models as to whether analysis proceeds from the bottom to the top or from the top to the bottom, the stratificatimal approach, like the tagmemic and PS views, sees the issue as a false one. In fact, Lamb (1966:6– 7) sums up the controversy in the context of linguistic history thusly:

> It is customary, and perhaps easiest, for linguistic analysis to start at or near the bottom of linguistic structure (i.e. in the phonology) and to work upwards. In the past it has often been thought that linguistic analysis *must* proceed in a series of orderly steps from the bottom upwards, and that it must follow a prescribed procedure; but demands of this type are too severe and are unnecessary. There is no necessity of doing a complete analysis at one level before going on to the next. If the analyst desires to attempt only a very rough analysis of one level before starting to work on the next higher one, and then to revise his preliminary analysis on the basis of what he learns from his examination of the higher stratum, he should feel free to do so. The structure of a language is an integrated whole with close interrelationships among neighboring subsystems, and therefore one can hardly be sure about the correctness of his solution for one subsystem of the language until the analysis of neighboring subsystems has been done. Thus, the analyst must be allowed to revise his solution in one area after working on a higher level. And why should one want to prevent him from doing so? Those not familiar with the history of linguistics during the forties and fifties may well wonder why. But it happens that there was a widely held view that a linguistic description should not be considered valid unless it could be shown that it was arrived at or could have been arrived at by the application of a mechanical step-by-step procedure. As a result, much linguistic theory of the forties and fifties consisted of attempts to devise such mechanical procedure (none of which were successful). The motivation for such stringency was that it provided a means of satisfying the important requirement that linguistic analysis be based on such principles that any (competent) independent investigator applying them to the same data would arrive at an equivalent solution. What was overlooked by most linguists during this period was that there is another far simpler way of meeting this requirement. It is to have the criteria for linguistic descrip-

tion stated simply as specifications which a linguistic description must meet. Criteria of this type are to be used for testing proposed descriptions rather than for prescribing procedures of analysis. Such criteria specify the properties of an acceptable solution. With this approach, the analyst has much greater freedom. He can jump around from one level of analysis to another at will. He can use meaning whenever he wants (notwithstanding earlier teachings to the contrary). He may also use intuition, hunches, and trial-and-error techniques. But when he arrives at a description, he must subject it to the test. In actual practice, he will be keeping the testing criteria in mind all along as he conducts his analysis, performing it so that the requirements will be satisfied. This approach does not in any way deny the value of various valuable analytical tools and techniques which a linguist should know; but these belong to the practical side of linguistics rather than to linguistic theory.

In a stratificational grammar there are networks and realization rules set up to describe languages. Relationships among levels occur as networks in which connections are made according to realization rules in what Lamb calls REALIZATIONAL ANALYSIS.

According to Lamb, the stratificationalist finds it convenient to distinguish two general types of linguistic analysis concerned with two kinds of linguistic patterning – tactic analysis and realizational analysis.

TACTIC ANALYSIS is the "process of isolating recurrent partial similarities." (Lamb 1966:5) This process is quite similar to the procedure for identifying morphemes using an abbreviated form of IA analysis. That is, given a body of data, it is possible to describe items in classes which co-occur instead of listing each item in each occurrence as would be done in an unabbreviated IA analysis. A simple tactic analysis of the following data will exemplify this point:

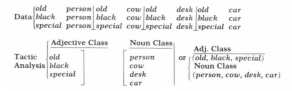

An IA morphemic analysis would reproduce the data in a list. Conversely, tactic analysis groups form into co-occurring classes in their positions of occurrence with respect to each other. Tactic analysis involves "little more than applying a simple factoring operation like that performed by the ninth-grade algebra student." (*ibid.*: 5)

Tactic analysis takes the description up to the level of what is IC analysis in the descriptive linguistic framework. But in stratificational grammar, "the determination of the immediate constituents of sentences, phrases, and words is of course not important as an end in itself; rather, such determination is an approach to the description of the tactic pattern of a stratal system." (*ibid.*: 54)

Every cut in an IC analysis, in tactic analysis is what stratificationalists refer to as a downward and in the tactic pattern. To illustrate this, consider Lamb's example of the analysis of the English word *untruly*. There are three possible ways cuts may be made: *un/true-ly, un/true/ly, untrue/ly*. The diagrams on page 118 represent the analyses respectively. They also show the notational form of a tactic analyses of *untruly*,

> The choice among the alternatives depends upon how they fit into the tactic description, which must of course account for other forms as well, in particular such forms as *truly* and *untrue*, and for the fact that the distribution of *true, untrue, wise, unwise*, etc. is different from that of *truly, untruly, wisely, unwisely*, etc. . .

> Diagram (1), for the analysis (un) (true ly), has quite obvious excess information whose elimination results in diagram (2), representing the three-way cut. But (2) can be further simplified to (3). Thus the analysis (un true) (ly) fits the simplest tactic description, and is for that reason to be considered the correct immediate constituent analysis. (*ibid:* 54)

In a stratificational model, realizational analysis, rather than tactic analysis, is used. This involves a set of four operations: horizontal grouping, horizontal splitting, vertical splitting, vertical grouping. In realizational analysis, the purpose is to link the levels. Any body of data (as text) exists at all levels simultaneously. Therefore, in realizational analysis, process statements to the effect that an item at one level becomes some-

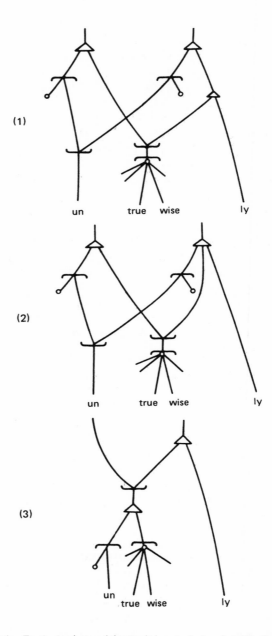

(1)

(2)

(3)

Alternative Tactic Analyses of the English *untruly* (Lamb 1966, fig. 26; 53)

thing else at another level do not occur. To clarify this point which is one of the main ones made by the stratificational approach, Algeo (1973:8–9) explained

> A process statement says that x becomes, or is changed into or is replaced by y, but, in a stratified grammar, x never disappears, is never changed into anything. X as a unit on one stratum may be realized as y on another stratum, but does not thereby disappear. Rather x remains as part of the structure of a text in its own stratal system.

The stratificational grammarian's rejection of process statements in an analysis largely derives from the type of data stratificationalists analyze. For example, rules of the type used in transformational/generative grammar are unacceptable in a stratificational analysis because they are "process formulations." According to Lamb (1971:104), "the now-famous transformational rule, was unacceptable to me since it was a process formulation, involving mutation of forms on the same level; and while such a formulation could apparently account for the primary data it was not realistic as applied to encoding and decoding."

Thus, the levels of grammar undergo tactic analysis such that the units at each level are identified and described as objective entities rather than processes. Then, all analyzed levels together are analyzed as a simultaneously occurring body of communicational behavior. Realizational analysis links the levels through grouping and splitting operations.

The end result of a stratificational analysis of a language conducted by examining the tactics and realization rules describable from the data is "a model of the information system that enables a person to speak his language" (*ibid.*: 99). This end result is particularly appropriate, given the goal of stratificational grammar as distinct from the goal we saw earlier for the beginning stages of PS grammar. For, as Sampson (1970: 11) notes:

> The main purpose of a stratificational grammar is not to generate all and only the utterances of the language in question, but rather to provide the correct realization for any content or expression structure which is appropriate for the language.

A major consideration of the stratificationalists and their model of linguistic analysis is the notion of *simplicity* as an evaluation measure. In tactic analysis, simplicity means stating units and their distribution with respect to each other algebraically rather than listing items and for each item identified stating its distribution in the text. In realizational analysis, the operations (grouping and splitting, horizontal and vertical)

> . . . are motivated by the simplicity principle and by the need to account for the linguistic data. Failure to carry one of them out, where the possibility is available, would mean either that the description would be failing to account for certain data or that it would be stating certain relationships repeatedly which might be stated only once. (Lamb 1966:6)

Stratificational grammar, then, in part is a model of grammatical description posited on a theory of description rather than on a set of discovery procedures. Stratificational theory describes a language as made up of subsystems and not as a single system in which basic units combine into more complex structures at successive levels. Thus, where in the descriptivist and early structuralist models, morphemes were described "as composed directly of phonemes," in a stratified description two subsystems are recognized each having its own phoneme and morpheme. Along with Lamb, H. A. Gleason, a staunch descriptivist, has been influential in recent years in developing this model. The stratified grammar proposed by Lamb and Gleason contains a language model consisting of three components each having two levels.

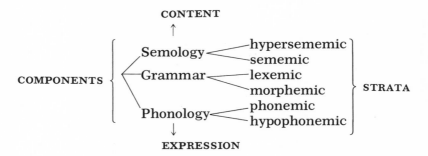

Each level is analyzed into minimal, emic units. The units at the hypophonemic level are distinctive features of sound such as nasality, labiality, and so on. At the phonemic level the units resemble Harris's morphophoneme. At the morphemic level, they are quite close to standard descriptively identified morphemes. Somewhat roughly, the units at each strata may be conceived of this way:

HYPERSEMEMIC—distinctive features of meaning—for example, animate, count, male, process, and so on.

SEMEMIC—idioms, complex words, and single morphemes which cannot be analyzed into smaller units without losing meaning.

LEXEMIC—the smallest units that enter into syntactic constructions.

MORPHEMIC—minimal units of sound combination with meaning.

PHONEMIC—minimal units of sound combination.

HYPOPHONEMIC—distinctive sound features.

The tactic rules "specify how the emes combine with one another" on each stratum while the realizational rules "describe how the emes of one stratum are linked to those of another." (Algeo 1973:7)

A stratificational analysis as an outgrowth of the structuralist formalist position further involves its own notational system for representing a stratified description of a language. Before we can provide an example of a stratificational analysis, it is necessary to give some consideration to this notational framework. Basically, it consists of

> quasi-circuitry diagrams consisting entirely of lines and nodes of various kinds. The diagrams are equivalent to formulas or "normal" English as a means of expressing grammatical relationships. And since diagrams, formulas, and "normal" English are equivalent ways of expressing a grammar, the choice between them depends on convenience and prejudice. (Algeo 1973:10)

Lamb (1966:41) favored the use of his line and node diagrams to represent a grammatical description in the interest of arriving at a successful evaluation procedure in terms of what he calls *effective information* conveyed by competing descriptions. To him,

> . . . a linguistic description conveys certain effective information about a linguistic structure, and to do so it uses a certain amount of surface information. In describing (part of) a linguistic structure the grammarian should try to present a maximum of effective information with a minimum of surface information. There are various operations which can be performed upon a preliminary or tentative description to simplify it, i.e. to reduce its surface information without alteration of its effective information. Two descriptions convey the same effective information if they account for (or predict) the same data.

An example of the stratificational use of network diagrams in realizational analysis to convey with minimal surface information maximal effective information about the structure of English is provided by Bolinger (1975:534) adapted from Lamb (1974:196a). In the diagram we further adapt that example. The following is a "model" of language description and a theory of language as communication.

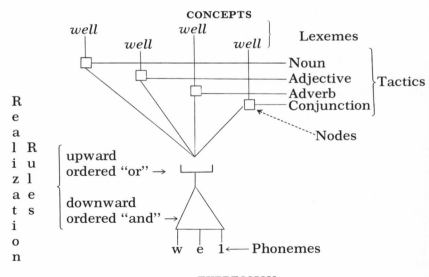

Of this example, Bolinger (1975:553–34) states

> The network concept can be seen . . . showing *well* connect-
> ed downward to phonemes and upward to lexemes (*well* as
> a hole in the ground and *well* as in interjection, among other
> examples), with each of the latter having an intersecting
> *node* with a particular tactic category (the hole in the ground
> is a noun, the *well* in *he writes well* is an adverb, and so on).

Lamb's diagrams are not meant to describe an entire language and all its subsystems as the number of lines and nodes
needed would be prohibitive. Yet, he feels that diagrams "en-
hance the clarity and readability of a description." He contends, however, that grammatical description should be in a
different form following certain conventions. Briefly illustrated, consider the following formula:

$$
\begin{array}{lll}
\text{LN} & \text{M} & \text{LN} = \text{lexon} \\
\textit{good} \quad |\ |\ \underline{\quad} \ (\text{er, est}) \ / \quad \text{beT} & & \text{M} = \text{morpheme} \\
+ \quad |\ |\ \underline{\quad} \ / \ \text{M} & & \\
\text{gud} & &
\end{array}
$$

> A formula of this type may be a REALIZATION RULE. It states
> that the structural relationships associated with ^{LN}/good/ are
> such that the realization ^{M}/beT/ occurs only when the compar-
> ative suffix or the superlative suffix follows; otherwise, i.e., in
> any other environment the realization ^{M}/gud/ occurs. (Lamb
> 1966:56)

Therefore, in a realization rule an eme (that is, an emic unit) of
the lexical strata ^{LN}/good/ is linked to emes (that is, emic units)
of the morphological strata, that is — ^{M}/bet/ and ^{M}/gud/.

In its claims to handle synonymy and homonymy, stratificational grammar goes further than previous models of grammatical description. One of its major differences from other
models or theories is its scope in seeking to account "not
merely for sentences, but also for texts of larger extent: para-
graphs, narratives, sonnets, five-act tragedies, epics, and the
Encyclopedia Britannica, any text that has formal unity."
While rejecting process statements in actual grammatical description in favor of stratal interconnections through networks

as realizations, stratificational grammar is proposed as "a model for the very process" of language itself. (Algeo 1974:10)

An important aspect of stratificational grammar is its method for describing meaning at the lexemic, sememic, and hypersememic levels. Here is a simple illustration of the sememic analysis of the concept and expression which results in the various lexical items in English which may be used for *father*.

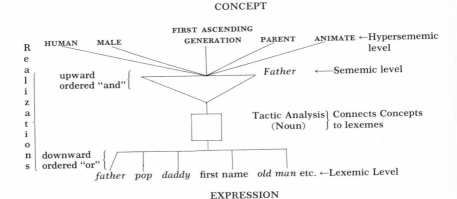

Adapted from a suggestion by Roberta Reeder.

This type of analysis combines that of stating hierarchical relationships among levels with the analysis of units at each level into components.

On the concept side of language where previous models of grammatical description have had little success, Lamb has been able to tie into his model what anthropologists who are interested in language employ—the approach of COMPONENTIAL ANALYSIS. Componential analysis, also known as formal semantic analysis, involves analyzing lexical items into their semantic components. For example, kinship terms in English can be broken into a limited number of component parts with each term specified by the combination of those features. The dimensions of sex of relative, generation, and lineality are sufficient to distinguish most, if not all, American kinship terms. In this way, *father* can be defined as male, one generation above ego, and lineal (ancestor of ego), while the components of the term *grandmother* can be stated as female, two generations above ego, and lineal. (Wallace and Atkins 1960:61)

Many proponents of componential analysis claim that their results reveal how people think, that the features of meaning have "psychological reality." In Lamb's theory, then, the linkage of levels from the sememic to the phonemic (if componential analysis reveals meaning) might be considered a theory of understanding language. However, there is considerable debate in anthropology and general linguistics as to whether or not componential analysis reveals or imposes conceptual categories on language. In fact, this raises the issue of the relationship of language to thought at any level — an issue for which no empirical solution seems to be in sight.

Lamb recognizes the need to include ideas about the world in a linguistic theory and suggests that his hypersememic tactic level might be accorded "a special status," considered "outside the language proper," and given "a more fitting name than the awkward term 'hypersememic.'" With this recognition Lamb (1971:119–20) recently rethought the hypersememic level and stated

> Accordingly I now call it the *conceptual system,* or for those who would like another Greek term, the *gnostemic* system; its basic units are the *gnosteme* and the *gnoston.* The gnoston is an elementary unit of knowledge, and this position in the system corresponds well to its Greek meaning, "something which is known."

Tagmemics furthered the descriptive approach to linguistic data by providing a discovery procedure for isolating the tagmeme as a basic unit of syntax. Lamb now suggests that it may be possible to discover basic units of knowledge as well as basic units of lexical and grammatical meaning above the morpheme.

Linguistic Theory of Language

We concluded our earlier discussion of structuralism by pointing out how structuralist approaches led, along with infusions from mathematics, to the development of PS grammar. PS grammar with its "new" and "better" way of handling syntax than IC analysis represents the beginning of TG grammar, a prevailing theory in linguistics today. It is generally thought that there are three general stages in the development of TG theory—the Syntactic Structures period, the "Aspects" period, and the lexicalist versus transformationalist period.

According to Allen and Van Buren (1971:ix), the main purpose of research in TG theory is "to suggest an explanatory hypothesis concerning the nature of language and ultimately of human thought." Therefore, data are not of interest in and of themselves but provide evidence of underlying "organizing principles in the mind which make it possible for a speaker to use language creatively." (*ibid.*)

A grammar in this theoretical framework is not an account of the data in a speech or text but a formal theory dealing with the rules whereby sentences are constructed forming sound and meaning relationships. The linguist's task is to formulate such rules that generate sentences and interrelate them as interpretable both phonetically and semantically. So far, this sounds in keeping with the call of the structuralists, particularly Zellig Harris, for a formal theory of the structure of language. In fact, this concept of formal theory is what Chomsky attempted by adding the notion of transformation to a PS grammar.

To Chomsky (1971:6) the task of rule formulation was seen to be "not of interest in itself but only insofar as it sheds light on the more general question of the nature of language." The nature of language which the theory hopes to explain is held to be universal. As such,

> . . . a general theory of this sort itself must provide a hypothesis concerning innate intellectual structure of sufficient richness to account for the fact that the child acquires a given grammar on the basis of the data available to him. More generally, both a grammar of a particular language and a general theory of language are of interest primarily because of the insight they provide concerning the nature of mental processes, the mechanisms of perception and production, and the mechanisms by which knowledge is acquired. (*ibid.*)

In this framework a grammar, in addition to being a theory of rule construction, is meant to be an account of linguistic *competence* and should therefore describe and account for "the ability of a speaker to understand an arbitrary sentence of his language and to produce an appropriate sentence on a given occasion." (*ibid.:* 7) The crucial point here is that linguistic theory and its conception of grammar have the intent of describing a completely different entity than linguistic description does. A grammar produced within any of the models of grammatical or language description discussed earlier is a description of language(s) as use. Generally, the models of language description are for describing speech or text. The linguistic theorists refer to speech and textual data as *performance* as distinct from competence. For linguistic theory this distinction between competence and performance is as crucial as the distinction between *langue* and *parole* is for structural linguistics. Chomsky (1971:29) put it this way:

> . . . it should be clearly recognized that a grammar is not a description of the performance of the speaker, but rather of his linguistic competence, and that a description of competence and a description of performance are different things.

The difference between competence and performance may be illustrated by an analogy suggested by Chomsky. Suppose a theory were devised to account for how a child learns to multiply. One would assume that once he has learned to multiply he is "competent." Yet when called on in class, his "performance" could vary from his level of competence. A description of the child's multiplication competence would be a statement "of some of the rules of arithmetic." A description of the child's performance, however, would involve information outside mathematics (for example, memory and likelihood of error) and competence descriptions would account for what is learned as multiplication regardless of how it is used.
In Chomsky's view,

> It seems clear that the description which is of greatest psychological relevance is the account of competence, not that of performance, both in the case of arithmetic and the case of lan-

guage. The deeper question concerns the kinds of structures the person has succeeded in mastering and internalizing, whether or not he utilizes them in practice without interference from the many other factors that play a role in actual behavior. For anyone concerned with intellectual processes, or any question that goes beyond mere data arranging, it is the question of competence that is fundamental. Obviously one can find out about competence only by studying performance, but this study must be carried out in devious and clever ways, if any serious result is to be obtained. (ibid.:*130*)

Chomsky (1971:131) strongly feels that transcribed linguistic data gathered from an informant "is almost useless as it stands, for linguistic analysis of any but the most superficial kind." Such vehemence, given linguistic theory conceived of as a grammar representing the knowledge humans have which allows them to acquire language, may be justified. However, for practitioners in language description where grammars are defined as descriptions of data for specific purposes the criticism may seem to be strong. No model of language description, in fact, purports to be aiming to provide a theory of performance. Ultimately this, too, is the task of linguistic theory, not language description.

Some linguists argue that TG, as a theory of language, seeks to explain both competence and performance. Chomsky contends that this distinction must be conceived of as a distinction specifically tied to the theory. The distinction is historically relatable to the langue/parole distinction made by deSaussure. However, it should be stressed here that "Chomsky rejects deSaussure's concept of langue as a systematic inventory of items and recommends that the linguist view underlying competence as a system of generative processes, as a system of rules accounting for language." (Eastman 1975:40) Thus, performance as the use of competence and *parole* as the individual expression of *langue* are also distinct insofar as competence/performance and *langue/parole* are paired distinctions within their respective linguistic models—that is, transformational/generative theory and structuralism respectively.

The "Aspects" Period

We have seen that, with the introduction of the idea of the transformation to a proposed model of language structure, accounting for certain types of structural ambiguity in sentences became possible. This accomplishment gave rise to a syntactic framework which seemed possible to be connected ultimately to the process of understanding sentences, a process which was thought to be explicable as a rule-governed system. The model of grammatical description in Chomsky's *Syntactic Structures* (1957) introduced the idea that syntax is the central component both in language description and linguistic theory. The prevailing idea behind the theory of language in the Syntactic Structures (henceforth, SS) framework was that the process of understanding sentences could be formally shown by reconstructing the representation of sentences at various structural levels, including the newly conceived of "transformational level where the kernel sentences underlying a given sentence can be thought of, in a sence [sic], as the 'elementary content elements' out of which this sentence is constructed." (1957:107–8) Certain transformational rules in a grammar applied to kernel sentences obligatorily and others optionally.

In his post-1957 writings, Chomsky added a rationalist dimension to his writings by focusing on the goal of producing a theory of linguistic structure. He thought this was necessary if linguists ever hoped to achieve a formal theory of language structure. Influenced by the French philosopher René Descartes, Chomsky observed that a creative aspect underlies the actual use of language. Whereas language description centers on describing the mechanical principles of language, linguistic theory ought to account as well for the "creative principle" of language. (Chomsky 1966:6)

In his *Aspects of the Theory of Syntax* (1965:59), Chomsky introduced a new period of TG theory. In this version of linguistic theory, we see that the goal of linguistics is to describe the "creative principle" of language, assuming that *all languages* share "general features of grammatical structure" and *all languages* "reflect certain fundamental properties of the mind."

In the "Aspects" theoretical model, we see that transformational grammar as a theory of language is replaced by generative grammar as a theory of language. In the "Aspects" model of grammar is still (as it was in the SS model) a theory of language, but between models the definition of grammar was changed. In the "Aspects" model,

> a grammar of a language purports to be a description of the ideal speaker-hearer's intrinsic competence. If the grammar is, furthermore, perfectly explicit—in other words, if it does not rely on the intelligence of the understanding reader but rather provides an explicit analysis of his contribution—we may (somewhat redundantly) call it a *generative grammar*. (Chomsky 1965:4)

During the Syntactic Structures period a grammar was defined as "a device that generates all of the grammatical sequences of L and none of the ungrammatical ones." (1957:13) The word generative may be seen to apply to the grammar in the SS model since it refers to describing relationships among elements of language structure dynamically. Phase structure rules of the form ($S \rightarrow NP + VP$) are generative. Since both stages of the theory (SS and "Aspects") employ generative rules and transformations, despite the fact that the theory was first known as transformational and then generative grammar, it has become common to refer to the theory wholly as transformational/generative (TG).

In the previous section on stratificational grammar we noted an antipathy toward the use of process statements or by extension the use of generative rules. This may be seen as a reflection of the purpose of language description versus theory. In a generative grammar a sentence is generated by a series of rules, and the rule-governed system is conceived of as a dynamic model. In a stratificational grammar, the goal is to describe the units or elements discoverable in actual sentences at different levels of grammar. To use process statements to accomplish this would occasion the loss of the very distinctions being made. Bolinger (1975:535) saw this and stated:

> There are two ways of describing a language, both as old as grammar itself. One is static; it assumes entities that are ar-

ranged in relation to one another. Stratificational grammar is a static model: it displays a set of items that can interchange under certain conditions. The other approach is dynamic: a verb conjugation, for example, is viewed as a process of *adding* endings to a stem.

In addition to being more rationalistically based and theoretically (rather than data-based and methodologically) oriented, the "Aspects" period of TG grammar introduced a new notion to linguistic theory—*deep structure*. We saw in our discussion of the SS model that both optional and obligatory transformational rules were proposed to operate on the output of phrase structure rules (kernel sentences). This essentially was *the* theory of language in Chomsky's *Syntactic Structures* (1957). However, it was never clear as to how one might keep the line between optional and obligatory transformations straight. (Bolinger 1975:537) In our previous discussion of the early stages of TG grammar an example of the passive transformation was given. Such a transformation allowed base or kernel sentences to be "transformed" into other sentences—different but clearly related by the statable transformational relationship. In that early SS model, for example, an active sentence generated by the PS rules could be transformed into the "same" sentence *but* passive or negative, and so on. However, other transformations were conceived of as rules to account for different possible interpretations of ambiguous sentences, given different structural analyses of the relationships of elements (or categories such as NP) in the sentence. Our example of this other type of transformation was the sentence generated by a set of PS rules, *Flying planes can be dangerous*. If the PS rules generated a kernel sentence with an NP as subject (that is, *Flying planes*), an optional transformation would account for the "other" reading on structural grounds (that is, *It can be dangerous to fly planes*). However, as these examples also show, it is not clear what determines which of a set of "related" sentences is generated by the PS rules. What logic is there to kernel sentences considered as active and inherently ambiguous? Could anyone really distinguish optional from obligatory transformations as significant to TG theory?

In 1964, linguists Katz and Postal, followers of Chomsky,

fórmulated a principle in response to the problems raised by early notions of grammatical transformations, claiming that *"the only contribution of transformations to semantic interpretations is that they interrelate Phrase-Makers."* (italics by Chomsky) (Chomsky 1965:132) From this came the principle in TG theory that transformations cannot introduce or delete "meaning-bearing" elements. The effect of this was to alter the framework of the theory radically: where in the SS model, a set of PS rules generated a kernel sentence which underwent transformations; in the "Aspects" model, a set of *base* rules generate a *"generalized Phrase-Marker."*

> A generalized Phrase-Marker formed in this way contains all of the base Phrase-Markers that constitute the basis of a sentence, but it contains more information than a basis in the old sense since it also indicates explicitly how these base Phrase-Markers are embedded in one another. That is, the generalized Phrase-Marker contains all of the information contained in the basis, as well as the information provided by the generalized embedding transformations. (*ibid.*:134)

So, in the "Aspects" model, syntax is conceived of as analyzing sentences as generated by a set of base rules in what is called the *base component*. The rules of the base component are of the early PS variety. But, in addition they also include information to account for more complex sentences (for example, embedded sentences). These rules of the base syntactic component generate a generalized phrase marker. The generalized phrase marker may also be called the "deep structure generated by the syntactic component." (*ibid.* :135)

> Thus the syntactic component consists of a base that generates deep structures and a transformational part that maps them onto surface structures. The deep structure of a sentence is submitted to the semantic component for semantic interpretation, and its surface structure enters the phonological component and undergoes phonetic interpretation. The final effect of a grammar, then, is to relate a semantic interpretation to a phonetic representation — that is, to state how a sentence is interpreted. This relation is mediated by the syntactic component of the grammar, which constitutes its sole "creative part." (*ibid.*:135 – 36)

Schematically, the "Aspects" model of a grammar as a theory of language might be envisioned thusly:

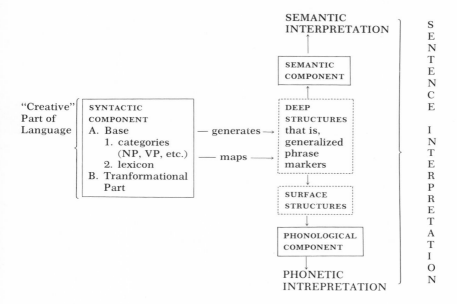

In this diagram, it should be noticed that the base of the syntactic component has two parts:

A "categorical subcomponent" which "consists of a sequence of context-free rewriting rules." (*ibid.:* 141) This is similar to a PS grammar and its rules in rewrite form (S → NP + VP, i.e., a sentence is rewritten as a Noun Phrase + a Verb Phrase) A lexicon which "consists of an unordered set of lexical entries and certain redundancy rules." (*ibid.*) The lexicon contains entries envisioned as phonological, syntactic, and semantic features. The redundancy rules "add and specify features wherever this can be predicted by general rule." (*ibid.:* 142) According to Chomsky, "the lexical entries constitute the full set of irregularities of the language."

The transformational part of the syntactic component consists of rules of substitution, deletions, and adjunctions applied to generalized phrase markers (deep structures), mapping them into surface structures. Bolinger (1975:538–39) provides an example of the "Aspects theory" in operation with the sentence *Did Rome conquer the barbarians?* In a modified, simplified form, the "Aspects" model which would account for that sentence might look like this:

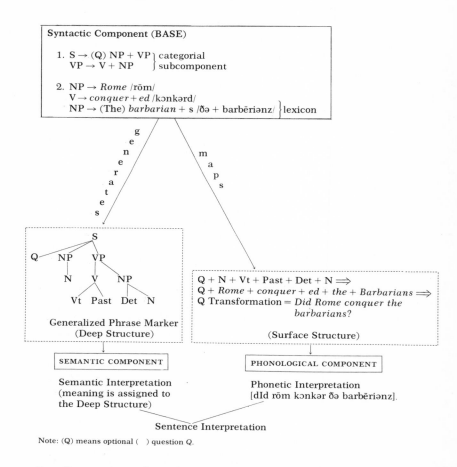

Note: (Q) means optional (   ) question Q.

In discussing the theoretical claims this model makes, Chomsky (1965:140) said:

> It would clearly be absurd to suppose that the "speaker" of such a language, in formulating an "utterance," first selects

the major categories, then the categories into which these are analyzed, and so forth, finally, at the end of the process, selecting the words or symbols that he is going to use (deciding what he is going to talk about). To think of a generative grammar in these terms is to take it to be a model of performance rather than a model of competence, thus totally misconceiving its nature. One can study models of performance that incorporate generative grammars, and some results have been achieved in such studies. But a generative grammar as it stands is no more a model of the speaker than it is a model of the hearer. Rather, as has been repeatedly emphasized, it can be regarded only as a characterization of the intrinsic tacit knowledge or competence that underlies actual performance.

Just as the "Aspects" model and the concept of deep structure modified the formal aspects of a proposed theory of linguistic competence, in the years since 1965 further changes have been made. Particularly significant since 1965 has been the debate in linguistic theory between the lexicalists and the transformationalists.

We saw that one of the main features of the "aspects" model was the advent in syntax of a deep structure generated by rules in a base component. The rules in the base component were conceived of as two types: categorial context-free rewrite rules and lexical redundancy rules. The next stage of linguistic theory was sparked by a controversy revolving around the question as to whether or not the lexicon belongs in a syntactic component. Questions arose also as to whether or not a level of deep structure should be posited, and if so, what did it add to a theory of language? *Lexicalists* defended the "Aspects" model while *transformationalists*, former adherents to the "Aspects" model, advocated abandoning deep structure. The post-"Aspects" model of TG theory has two branches: one group of scholars advocates *generative semantics;* the other propounds the *extended standard theory.*

Again, developments in theory, as well as developments in language description, may be seen to occur where previous formulations have proved unsatisfactory in certain ways. The "Aspects" model has been now dubbed the "standard theory."

At both the SS and "Aspects" stages of linguistic theory, syntax was the focus of the theory. With "Aspects" we saw the addition of the lexicon to the syntactic base. Jerrold Katz and Jerry Fodor (1964), whose work preceded Chomsky's *Aspects of the Theory of Syntax,* advanced the theory that linguistic description minus grammar equals semantics. Their semantic theory begged the issue of where syntax might end and semantics begin. With lexical entries and redundancy rules posited in the syntactic component in the "Aspects" model (that is, in the base), some linguists concluded that the distinction was an artificial one, especially given the notion of a deep structure as generated by both categorial rules (containing NP, VP, PRO, and so on) and lexical rules (using "meaning" features, such as [animate], [mass]). Katz and Fodor (and Chomsky) attempted to refute such criticism by arguing strongly that syntax is autonomous. However, having expanded the domain of linguistics to include semantics, their position became difficult to defend. Katz and Fodor claimed that in the semantic component, semantic representations may be formally depicted with labeled trees just as deep structure in syntax consists of labeled trees. Moreover, they contended that the semantic component of a TG grammar included a *dictionary* of lexical items, a set of *projection rules* which "operates on full grammatical descriptions of sentences and on dictionary entries to produce semantic interpretations for every sentence of the language." (1964:493) In their view, semantic interpretation of a sentence involves assigning each lexical formative in a syntactic string its meanings from the dictionary. The meanings are then combined by the projection rules according to the sentence's structural description.

> The projection rules operate in the following way: the syntactic component provides the semantic component with a sentence like *the man hit the ball*. With this sentence is associated the appropriate structural description. First, the semantic component assigns the semantic interpretations to each lexical item. These interpretations are compatible with the syntactic markers of each lexical item (for example, *hit* as a verb, not as a noun) both in the dictionary entry and in the structural description. The semantic readings can be called EXPANDED in the sense that to the dictionary meanings are added, for

each lexical item, the meanings each item acquires through its syntactic relations. The expanded readings are then combined to form derived readings, and these in turn are combined until derived readings are obtained that express the meaning of the whole sentence. In this process meanings will be assigned to *the, man, "past," hit, the, ball;* they will be expanded in terms of the immediate constituent relations, for example, of *the man* and *hit the ball,* but not for substrings like *the man hit* or *hit the.* The derived meanings of *the man* and *hit the ball* can then be combined to produce the derived meaning of *the man hit the ball.* (Dinneen 1967:392)

In 1971, George Lakoff broke with such claims of the standard theory as propounded in the "Aspects" model by proposing the theory of generative semantics. He argued that maintaining a distinction between syntax and semantics by forcing differences (such as that of lexicon versus dictionary and deep structure versus semantic representation) was counterproductive in a theory of language. His position is called a transformationalist one while Chomsky's, because of insistence on positing a lexicon in the syntactic component, is called lexicalist. In brief, Lakoff's view claimed that "semantic representations and syntactic phrase markers [deep structure] are formal objects of the same kind, and that there exist no projection rules, but only grammatical transformations." (Lakoff 1971:269)

Lakoff's theory of generative semantics holds that a grammar as a theory of language is a system of rules which relate sound in language to meaning. In Lakoff's scheme, semantic representations and phonological representations of sentences result in a language-independent way. Moreover, "the lexicon contains the necessary phonological semantic, and syntactic information in order for the lexical items to be interpreted in a sentence." (Eastman 1975:108) Thus, given a sentence's syntactic structure, semantic representation involves linking the syntactic string to a set of *presuppositions* about the world and relating to notions such as the sentence's *topic* and *focus.* The actual machinery involved in relating and defining presuppositions, topic, focus, and the like within the theory need to be worked out – a main area of current research. The theory of generative semantics in its current stage claims that a theory of linguistic competence contains a semantic component such that a sentence's semantic representation represents the inherent logical form of the sentence.

Basically, generative semantics suggests that sentences in a theory of language can be interpreted by a set of rules which relate meaning to speech without having to posit a level of syntactic deep structure. As Bolinger put it (1975:542): "The generation of a sentence does not start with a syntactic structure but with a structured meaning, called the remote structure, which all the rules together then convert to a surface structure."

While maintaining his lexicalist stance despite the criticisms of the transformationalists, Chomsky has recently modified his "standard" theory of linguistic competence as presented in *Aspects*. In lectures at McMaster University in 1975, he unveiled his more recent position, which is actually the standard theory extended. The lectures, somewhat elaborated, constitute Part 1 of a book entitled *Reflections on Language* (Chomsky 1975) from which we will quote liberally in order to present the precise views of that version of the theory.

A major revision in Chomsky's thinking has brought him closer to the generative semanticists regarding the deep structure issue. For example,

> In the so-called "standard theory," the initial phrase markers were called "deep structures" but I will avoid the term here, for several reasons. In the standard theory, deep structures were characterized in terms of two properties: their role in syntax, initiating transformational derivations; and their role in semantic interpretation. As for the latter, it was postulated that deep structures give all the information required for determining the meaning of sentences. Clearly, these characterizations are independent; it might turn out that the structures that initiate transformational derivations are not those that determine semantic interpretation. I believe that this is the case. The "extended standard theory" postulates that surface structures contribute in a definite way to semantic interpretation. (1975:81–82)

So while holding on to the necessity of transformational derivations through rules generated by the syntactic component,

Chomsky agrees that the rules of the syntactic component do not generate all the information necessary to interpret sentences meaningfully in language. His position sees transformational rules as necessary in syntax yet, at the same time, concedes that sentence interpretation may be accomplished in a linguistic theory by more reference to surface rather than deep structures. Stressing this, he states:

> I will suggest that perhaps all semantic information is determined by a somewhat enriched notion of surface structure. In this theory, then, the syntactic and semantic properties of the former "deep structure" are dissociated. Either class of properties might, then, be taken as defining the technical notion of "deep structure." To avoid the issue, with the possible attendant confusion, I will simply drop the term, speaking only of "initial phrase markers" and "surface structures." (*ibid.*:82)

Still, in this model, as the diagram of the "Aspects" model shows, the syntactic base component, however constituted, generates phrase markers which are mapped onto surface structures. This model like the "Aspects" model differs from the generative semantics proposal in retaining the central position of syntax in a theory of language. The extended standard theory holds that what should be done is to "enrich the notion of surface structure" so that sentential meaning may be determined "under interpretive rules." (*ibid.*:83) In this view phrase markers generated by the syntactic base only indirectly determine the structures that are semantically interpreted. Instead semantic interpretation is more directly accomplished through surface structure.

The proposed extended standard theory aims to develop a "theory of semantic interpretation of surface structures." (*ibid.*:95) One of the postulates involved is that the notion of "surface structure" is altered so that in this newer model "*only* surface structures undergo semantic interpretation." Part of the extended notion of surface structure which is a significant part of the extended standard theory is the *trace theory of movement rules.*

Chomsky (1976:33) expresses the philosophy underlying his latest formulation of theory thusly:

The child learning English simply imposes the requirement that mentally present subjects function as though they were physically present. He does this even in the absence of relevant evidence, so it appears a theory of universal grammar — that is, a theory of the language facility — must seek an explanation as to why this is so. The answer, I think, lies in the "trace theory of movement rules," which requires that when a phrase is moved by transformation it leaves behind a phonetically null but morphologically real element "trace" (a so-called "zero morpheme") that functions semantically as a kind of bound variable. Other rules of syntax and morphology have no way of knowing that this element will (ultimately) be phonetically null. Hence it operates as a specified subject, and in other ways in the system of rules, while playing an essential role in semantic interpretation.

Evidence of trace may be seen in the following interrogative sentences suggested by Chomsky:

1. *Who do you want to hit* ← from ⎰*You want to hit who*
2. *Who do you want to see Bill* ← ⎱*You want who to see Bill*
3. *Who do you want to choose* ←⎰a. *You want who to choose*
                                   ⎱b. *You want to choose who*

Sentence 3 is ambiguous. In trace theory, abstract structures may be set up for 1, 2, 3 as follows:

    1' *Who do you want to hit* t
    2' *Who do you want* t *to see Bill*
    3' a. *Who do you want* t *to choose*
       b. *Who do you want to choose* t

In each abstract structure, t is the trace left by the movement of *who* from the sentences from which 1, 2, 3 respectively derive. Where each t occurs in the abstract structures (as replacing *who* in the underlying sentences) a rule for English which links *want* and *to* when they co-occur is blocked because of the intervening t (marking where *who* was in the underlying form).

The rule is the one which exists for some English speakers in which *want* + *to* → *wanna*. Thus,

       1' *Who do you wanna hit t*
       2' *Who do you want t to see Bill*
       3' a. *Who do you want t to choose*
           b. *Who do you wanna choose t*

Thus, 2' and 3'a are interpreted such that the answer to them both is a person — that is, *I want Sam to see Bill; I want Sam to choose.* Likewise, 3b. would be answered, *I want to choose Sam.*

> Although the trace is phonetically null [in 1, 2, 3], it is syntactically and morphologically real and enters into the computations that determine the form and meaning of sentences. (1976:54)

Moreover, the trace theory of movement rules holds that it is possible to get around questions of a sentence's syntactic or semantic acceptability by deriving the "logical form" of the "sentences in question from surface structures in which trace appears." (*ibid.:*95). Chomsky uses the following example (paraphrased from *ibid.:*93–94),

a. Surface structure: *the police know who the FBI discovered that Bill shot.*
b. Logical form: *the police know (for which person) the FBI discovered that Bill shot x.*

The logical form contains a variable x and a quantifier "for which x." It is said that the quantifier *binds* the variable. Now, in trace theory, Chomsky suggests that the variable x is identified with a trace t left by the syntactic rule which moved the quantifier in the grammatical and semantically interpretable surface structure sentence (that is, a). Thus, the derivation of the surface structure a from its logical form could be represented as c.

c. Sentence 1 *the police know*
   Sentence 2 *(who) the FBI discovered* – quantifier *(who)*
   Sentence 3 *that Bill shot* (t) – trace (t) of moved quantifier
         (who)

To convert c to its logical form (b) "all that is required is the information that 'who' is a quantifier binding t and meaning 'for which person t' (*ibid.:* 94). Thus, the position of the bound quantifier in the surface structure aids in interpreting the sentence just as the trace of a quantifier which does not appear in the surface structure also does as we saw in the previous example.

Chomsky provides a number of additional motivations for devising the trace theory of movement rules. In all instances, traces of derivational rules forming a sentence's logical form are posited, as appearing in the surface structure, as aids to semantic interpretation. The extended standard theory incorporating the notion of trace holds that grammar as a theory of language has the following structure:

> The rules of the categorial component and the lexicon [see "Aspects" model diagram page 133] provide initial phrase markers. Applying transformations to these, we derive surface structures (including traces), which undergo semantic interpretation. The rules of semantic interpretation assign the scope of logical operators ("not", "each", "who", etc.) and fix their meaning, assign antecedents to such anaphoric expressions as reciprocals ("each other") and necessarily bound anaphors (e.g. "his" in "John lost his way", where "his" must refer to John, as contrasted with the unbound anaphor "his" in "John found his book," where "his" may refer to any male, including John). The result of application of these rules we may call a "logical form." (*ibid.:* 104)

Grammar in the extended standard theory is, as Chomsky claims, sentence grammar. Chomsky feels that sentence grammar in this extended standard theory is a "reasonable picture" of the general nature of a theory of language. Furthermore, he feels that it fits into "the system of cognitive structures." Schematically, the extended standard theory of TG grammar might be viewed as follows:

SENTENCE GRAMMAR

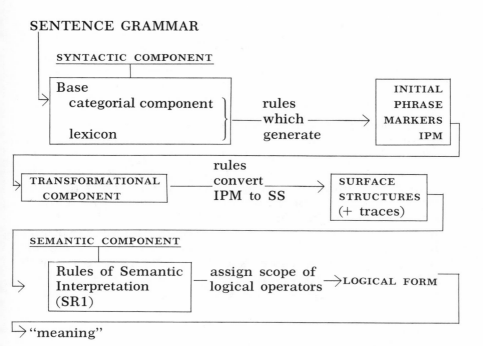

Beyond what the above diagram shows, Chomsky (*ibid.:* 105 claims that the logical forms generated by sentence grammar in order to be semantically interpreted must undergo "other semantic rules (SR2) interacting with other cognitive structures, giving fuller representations of meaning."

In what we have said about the extended standard theory we have only mentioned one of the principles used, that of trace theory. However, for our purposes, this incomplete discussion should serve to show that work on a theory of language has moved toward the idea that surface structures are what are semantically interpreted. Chomsky (*ibid.:*111) has also introduced ideas on how the principles of the extended standard theory tie in with the goals of linguistic theory.

> Principles of the sort that we have just been discussing are of considerable importance. They restrict the class of possible rules, and also the possible application of established rules.

Therefore, they contribute to solving the fundamental problem of linguistic theory, hence of "learning theory". . . . namely: to constrain the class of "learnable systems" so that it becomes possible to explain the rapidity, uniformity, and richness of learning within cognitive capacity . . . These are all steps towards what has been called "explanatory adequacy."

Furthermore, Chomsky (*ibid.*:118) feels that the principles of a theory of language developed in his extended theory and which "appear to have explanatory power for English are principles of universal grammar." He maintains that "on the assumption of uniformity of language capacity across the species, if a general principle is confirmed empirically for a given language, and if, furthermore, there is reason to believe that it is not learned (and surely not taught), then it is proper to postulate that the principle belongs to universal grammar, as part of the system of 'pre-existent knowledge' that makes learning possible." (*ibid.*:118)

Summary

The analysis of content has long presented problems to scholars interested in the description of language use — that is, use as evidenced by instances of speech. The descriptivists realized that their target of analysis, speech, consists of both content and expression. But they were hindered in their analysis by the fact that content did not afford them the useful basic units of analysis that expression did. Eventually tagmemicists, working within the descriptivist framework, seized upon ways to segment the content of speech as well. Gaining access to content as containing units of function in context, they analyzed lexemes in terms of the correlation of grammatical and situational roles.

Growing out of the structuralist interest in the grammatical system of particular languages, linguists working on machine translation began to see ways to analyze content as well. To machine translators content analysis entailed the preparation of dictionaries for particular languages with entries noting the function of an item correlated with its form. In the translation process like form and function in one language could be substituted for like form and function in another.

In addition to proposing to analyze content as well as expression (in the description of language as speech), and grammatical meaning as well as grammatical form (in the description of language as *langue*), linguists began using these models of language description for analyzing the facts of the encoding and decoding of language, now defined as communication.

Stratificationalists propose a formal model of the structure of language as communicative behavior. Tagmemicists make statements about the structure of "rational human communication."

The methods of a tagmemic analysis of a body of speech data involve the use of a basic unit of analysis at the level of grammar above the morpheme. This unit, the tagmeme, is composed of a slot specifying the grammatical function expressed (for example, S — subject) and a filler specifying what performs the grammatical function (for example, NP — noun phrase). Like the morpheme, the tagmeme is analyzed in terms of its distribution. Tagmemics furthered the scope of descriptive linguistics by proposing a discoverable basic unit of the analysis of syntactic expression in the description of a body of speech data. Tagmemics also signaled a breakthrough in the area of language description by providing the long-awaited unit of analysis to be used in analyzing content. Units analyzed in the feature mode may be considered units of content and are discoverable in a lexicon. They are minimal units of expression which occur in like contexts, thereby constituting units of contextual behavior: to the tagmemicists, the minimal units of the content side of language may be so behaviorally defined; therefore, the lexeme is a unit of function correlated with form.

Support for tagmemics as an approach to the analysis of speech data has recently come from an unexpected sphere. Charles Fillmore, a proponent of early TG grammar, in his attempt to analyze sentences in that framework, proposed a model known as *case grammar*. Unlike later transformationalists, he has remained a language describer where others have turned to designing models of linguistic competence. Case grammar is an attempt to solve "problems in a grammatical description of language phenomena." (Fillmore 1968:81) Both tagmemics and case grammar examine semantic category relationships to grammatical categories. Where the tagmeme +S: NP describes a subject slot (semantic category) filled by a noun phrase (grammatical category), case grammar further examines the relationships between the categories. Fillmore (*ibid.:* 5) contends that the case relationships (that is, agent, instrument, object, factitive, locative, benefactive) are "semantically relevant syntactic relationships involving nouns and the structures that contain them [and] that these relationships . . . are empirically discoverable. . . ." Thus, an NP filling a subject slot might have any of a number of semantic interpretations or functions as subjects. For example, agents as NPs may fill subject slots (John *had the house built*), as well as objects (*The* house *was built by John*), and instruments (*The* carpenter *built the house*). As Fillmore observes,

> There is an easy conversion from underlying representations of case grammar to "tagmemic" formulas . . . a case-grammar diagram could simply be read off as a tagmemic formula . . . One can as easily say "NP filling an A [Agent]" slot as anything else. (1968:88)

Recent work in tagmemics has accepted a number of Fillmore's ideas and has dealt with studying case relationships as they serve to relate situational roles (cases) to grammatical roles.

MT efforts looked to the description of the structural system of languages as a potential means of making it possible to translate from one language to another. Machine translators aimed to produce a definitional model of *langue* such that every language's *langue* would be explicitly and formally stated. Therefore, units and relationships could be interchanged or translated from one *langue* to another. Reflections of *langue* as *parole* in each language could be translated since the systematic relationships underlying the texts of each language could be stated.

For MT, the data need not necessarily be instances of speech elicited from an informant in a field setting. Because of the storage capacity of machines, vast texts of data could be stored and then analyzed together. MT was seen to involve eliminating differences in instances of expression in two languages by converting the differences to equivalences, thereby effecting translation.

As tagmemics began to make inroads on the analysis of content as well as expression in its proposed feature mode of analysis (discovering meaning in behavioral context), MT researchers, too, overcame the content barrier. Machine translators in the structuralist tradition began analyzing content by shifting from describing grammatical relationships to describing the function of such relationships as well. In MT, content was seen as function as opposed to structure (expression).

Both tagmemicists and machine translators continued to move away from descriptive linguistics in their ideas that the levels of content and expression (sound, grammar, meaning) in language are used simultaneously and should be described as co-occurring rather than separate.

The model of language description proposed by stratificationalists continued this way of thinking. The idea became widespread that it remained desirable for a description of a body of speech data to be based on principles which could be used by all linguists wishing to describe such data. However, keeping levels of descriptions entirely separate (with separate discovery procedures) in order to aid the linguist who *must* be able to show how a description was arrived at step by step was no longer considered necessary. The principles of analysis which could be used by other linguists for analyzing data could be stated as a set of "specifications which a linguistic description must meet." Such criteria could be used to evaluate or test a linguist's descriptions rather than prescribe analytical procedures.

With this notion, the new forms of descriptive linguistics as alternative methods and techniques of language description provided linguistics with the freedom to use common sense in solving analytical problems of describing language data. Postdescriptivist models of grammatical description increased the stock of discovery procedures available to the linguist as well as created units of analysis for the first time above the "level" of the morpheme. Linguists segmenting a body of speech data now have procedures for analyzing both expression (phoneme and morpheme) and content (tagmeme, lexeme, sememe, and perhaps even the gnosteme).

Parallel to such strides, in the 1960s a group of theoreticians working in TG grammar urged linguists to turn away from working on descriptive theory and to strive to explain language as knowledge. Linguists were urged to work toward developing a formal model of language acquisition as a general model of linguistic competence.

Where language description has been making inroads in the concerted effort to locate and describe units of the content side of language use, linguistics, in the theoretical sense, has involved efforts to provide a working model of intrinsic competence. Linguistic theorists have discovered that they need to deal with semantics just as language describers need to consider content.

As Fillmore's case grammar grew out of TG grammar and influenced tagmemics as a model of grammatical description, it also proved to be influential in early attempts by theorists to develop a model of the semantic component of a transformational/generative grammar.

In case grammar, the case relationships as agent, object, etc. of nouns (NPs) in sentences are "modeled on the predicate calculus of formal logic; in describing a sentence we look at the verb expression, which predicates something and who and what take part in it." (Bolinger 1975:547)

Case as a term refers to the type of involvement a person or subject has in an action. For example, consider the involvement of *He* in these sentences,

He *hit the ball*	Agent (personal)
He *received a blow*	Patient (recipient)
He *received a gift*	Beneficiary
He *loves her*	Affected Person
He *has black hair*	Interested Person
	(Fillmore 1968:6)

Fillmore's views make it possible to describe the semantic functions noun phrases have in relation to their verbs. The functions are describable from their deep structures.

To Fillmore, a sentence should be rewritten not as S → NP + VP and so on but as

S → M(modality) + P(proposition)
P → Predicate + Arguments
Arguments → Participants + Roles (cases)
Case → Agent, Instrument, Object, and so on.

Fillmore's grammar is essentially a reformulation of PS grammar. The *modality* category of a sentence refers to its grammatical features of tense, mood, and aspect which can be handled by regular PS rules. With the idea of the *proposition* as a major component of case grammar, it is possible for the first time to formally relate semantic functions (as evidenced by case) to syntactic functions.

> The generative semanticists acknowledge their debt to case grammar, and the similarity between the two approaches is apparent in the fact that both generate from functions (meanings) rather than from structural configurations. If case grammar had not acquired a separate label, it could just as easily be counted as a special version of generative semantics. (Bolinger 1975:550)

A current goal of theory is to develop a "theory of semantic interpretation of surface structures." (Chomsky 1975:95) A current goal of description is to describe the units of the content side of speech (or text) and the patterned relationships those units enter into with units at other descriptive levels of spoken (or textual) expression. If the sentence grammar of linguistic theory corresponds to a model of cognitive structure, then the theory of language would be sufficiently general to encompass the intuitions native speakers of particular languages have for their languages. Still, the speech of speakers of language — that is, their behavior or performance — for some purposes could not be described in an observationally adequate way by reference to any formal model of cognition. Although linguistic theory and language description remain separate tasks, each has made inroads in its most problematic area: the latter regarding content in description, the former concerning semantic interpretation in theory.

For Thought and Discussion

1. Define the phoneme as a unit in descriptive linguistics, tagmemics, and stratificational grammar. Is it the same in each approach to the analysis of language data? Summarize the importance of the notions etic and emic in the study of language and in the area of language description especially. Are etic and emic notions of any use in linguistic theory? If so, explain how and if not, why not?

2. Is it meaningful to compare Chomsky's *Syntactic Structures* model of grammatical description with his *Aspects of the Theory of Syntax*? If so, then explain what your comparison reveals. If not, contrast the approaches to language and summarize your conclusions. Hint: the words *structures* and *theory* in the book titles might provide direction for your answer.

3. Do you believe language is innate or learned? Compare this question about language to the debate in psychology as to whether heredity or environment is the determining factor in intelligence (you might consult a number of introductory psychology texts for help here). How do the arguments in psychology compare with those arguments linguists use who fall on either side? Would Kenneth Pike, for example, be on the environment or heredity side? Given questions of intelligence in psychology and of language in linguistics, do you believe that both language and intelligence can be usefully considered as *both* innate and learned? Would this be possible? What connection, if any, do you see between what linguists call "language" and what psychologists call "intelligence"?

4. We saw in this chapter that MT efforts were hindered because linguistics had not yet proceeded far enough in analyzing textual data in terms of its content. If we could not analyze the content of an utterance in both languages, how could we automatically translate from one to the other, since translation involves both content as well as form (expression)?

List some of the problems that you might imagine are involved in translating these English sentences to another language:

a. *She has been called to her final reward.*
b. *She is out of her misery.*
c. *She has been taken to paradise.*
d. *She has left us.*
e. *She has left a vacant chair.*
f. *She has shuffled off this mortal coil.*
g. *She has given up the ghost.*
h. *She has withdrawn in silence from the living.*
i. *She has met Life's last demand.*
j. *She has passed.*
k. *She has passed away.*
   (suggested in Pound [1936] as reprinted in Clark, Eschholz, and Rosa [1972:313–314])

Translate these sentences into a foreign language, if you know one. What happens? Think of at least five other sentences that "mean" the same thing. What do these sentences "mean" in English? Is the sentence *"She has died"* a translation of a–k? If so, how? And if not, how not?

What needs to be done with MT efforts to allow sentences like a–k which frequently occur in texts, to be translated from English to other languages?

5. How would both a generative semanticist and a standard theory supporter handle sentences a–k in question 4? How would they agree in their approach to the sentences? How would they disagree?

6. This question is quoted from Clark, Eschholz, and Rosa (1972:260).

> Many problems are encountered when a computer is used in language study. *Traddutore, tradittore* is an old Italian adage which means "the translator is a traitor" and indicates how subtle and difficult the translator's task is. Imagine the problems that arise when a computer is used for translation. For example, a computer translated "out of sight, out of mind" into Japanese and back into English as "invisible, insane." What happened in the process?

Be as specific in your answer as you can.

7. Why should most proposals for language description be opposed to process statements while proposals for linguistic theory should require them?

From what has been discussed so far, what is there about

what gets described as language versus what gets theorized about as language that makes this situation possible? To help you here, consider and remember that *concerning process statements*, Harris (1951:737), noted that elements which undergo processes "are seen as having histories, so that the relation of an element to sequences which contain it becomes the history of the element as it is subject to various processes and extensions." Such presentations of elements as engaging in processes are presentations of a system "which constitutes the description of the language structure."

8. Review what you have learned about structural linguistics (Chapter Two) and then consider each approach to language discussed in this chapter as it relates to structural linguistics in terms of: (1) object of description, (2) goals of description, (3) data being described, and (4) method and theory espoused.

In other words, be prepared to fill in the following matrix, justify each entry, and discuss how each approach is related to the others for each category being compared.

	Structural	Tagmemic	Stratification	MT	TG
object	langue				
goal	formal model				
data	speech				
method/theory	account for all and only utterances in a language				

FIVE

Language and Linguistics vis-à-vis Language Description

In this chapter we shall examine current and diverse research in language description and current and diverse research in linguistic theory. Two orientations to the scientific study of language reflect the distinction which has developed between theory and description. According to Bolinger (1975: vi), these views are language as an evolving capacity within the individual, and language as a means and product of social interaction.

The study of individual language capacity is also undertaken by scholars calling themselves PSYCHOLINGUISTS and by researchers working in a field called ARTIFICIAL INTELLIGENCE. In general, psycholinguistic research occurs alongside the work on linguistic theory with frequent interchanges of ideas among artificial intelligence researchers, psychologists and TG theorists.

Scholars calling themselves SOCIOLINGUISTS investigate language as a means and product of social interaction. Like language description, sociolinguistic research focuses on language use. Moreover, its goal is that of describing language as used in social contexts; therefore, much research is devoted to devising appropriate methods for the analysis and gathering of data.

Sociolinguists describe language as speech. In doing so, however, they move outside the body of data to consider social variables as well. In fact, Fishman (1968:5) defines sociolinguistics as the study of the "patterned covariation of language and society."

In this chapter, we will first survey the emerging fields of sociolinguistics and psycholinguistics as offshoots of language description and linguistic theory. Next we will examine the goals of linguistic description today. Finally, we will present the goals of linguistic theory now being sought by psycholinguists and theorists who attempt to understand language and the relationship of language and mind.

Bolinger (1975:5) predicts that the now-separated studies of language description and linguistic theory are moving toward reconciliation because

> Mind, inborn capacities, latent tendencies are not enough. There has to be a power that wakens and later guides them. That power is the social environment, with its expanding circles of family, playmates, school, and workaday associations, all shaping the child's inner drive for verbal expression.

Admittedly linguistic theory so far is attempting primarily to deal with linguistic competence. However, theoretical writings today reflect glimmers of a recognition that some directions in the study of language use may contribute to a theory of performance as part of a comprehensive theory of language. The rationalist bias of theory and the continued empirical basis of description, however, often work at cross purposes.

As we have observed in previous chapters, language use in the framework of theory is considered unexplainable until there is an explanatorily adequate theory of linguistic competence. Knowledge of language use has to be considered with the cognitive capacity of linguistic competence. As Chomsky (1975:36) maintains:

> The theory of language is simply that part of human psychology that is concerned with one particular "mental organ," human language. Stimulated by appropriate and continuing experience, the language faculty creates a grammar that generates sentences with formal and semantic properties. We say that a person knows the language generated by this grammar. Employing other related factors of mind and the structures they produce, he can then proceed to use the language he now knows.

This "mental organ," human language, is used by humans in social and personal interaction and can be described. Children may be observed acquiring language—that is, it is possible to transcribe and analyze the early stages of language as speech. And it is possible to analyze structurally speech and textual material. Chomsky agrees that empirical observations of such types of performance of language have value. In fact, he holds that the "study of structure, use, and acquisition may be expected to provide insight into essential features of language." (*ibid.*:56)

For linguistics to become a unified science, however, certain "old mysteries" need to be solved. Until such solutions are found, the science of linguistics will not be able to fully explain its object: language. We need to explain how rules of language are "accepted" by humans and how they are followed "to express our thoughts, our beliefs, our wishes, and so on." (*ibid.*: 75) It may be, as current research appears to be assuming, that the rules which are followed in language acquisition are different from the type of rules in language use.

> We must distinguish between the literal meaning of the linguistic expression produced by S and what S meant by producing this expression . . . The first notion is the one to be explained in the theory of language. The second has nothing particular to do with language . . . . (Chomsky 1975:76)

The second notion, however (that is, what S meant by producing an expression), has much to do with recent types of research in language description. It is not that linguistic theorists fail to recognize that the intent of an expression is related to language, rather they feel that to explain such an aspect of performance is beyond the scope of their field until an adequate theory of competence is available. In general, linguistic theorists remain skeptical of many approaches taken to analyze intent through the study of language use. This recognition by theorists and describers that common problems exist is a strong indication that linguistics is headed for ultimate unification. Linguistic theory attempts to explain the development of language as a cognitive structure (competence) and faces problems "to be solved, but not . . . impenetrable mysteries." Yet, theorists believe "the study of the capacity to use these structures and the exercise of this capacity, however, still seems to elude our understanding." (Chomsky 1975:77)

Research in Language Description

SOCIOLINGUISTICS, the main subfield of language description today, is the study of the use of language (speech, generally) in a number of social settings. Sociolinguists deal with the "use functions of language." They study language as a means and product of social interaction. In its concern for what speakers of languages or dialects need to know in order to communicate effectively in their cultures, sociolinguistics contributes toward an understanding of the relationship of language to culture at the level of performance. Currently, it is concerned with observational adequacy, attempting to describe the data of language in context.

Sociolinguistics embraces a number of types of study. Primarily, sociolinguistic descriptions of language use fall into one of two schools: one school is concerned with explaining communicative competence; the other centers on the understanding of contemporary linguistic change. Both approaches involve using certain methods for analyzing linguistic data in relation to the social and/or linguistic context in which it is used. On the one hand, the study of communicative competence is carried out by scholars focusing on social variables as related to language; on the other hand, the study of contemporary linguistic change is generally done by scholars focusing on linguistic variables as related to society.

Another type of language description based on the analysis of linguistic "speech" data can be seen in recent studies of animal communication. It should be noted at this point that there is a shift occurring in language description regarding the object of description. This new object of description ranges from communicative competence to nonverbal communicative behavior in humans and nonhumans.

The Description of Communicative Competence

COMMUNICATIVE COMPETENCE is "what a speaker needs to know to communicate effectively in culturally significant settings." (Gumperz and Hymes 1972:vii). Specialists in communicative competence deal with speech as behavior manifested by members of speech communities. Speakers, as individuals, use their speech to mark their social and self-identity and interact with other speakers in various cultural activities. These functions of speech are what communicative competence scholars describe to show how language is used appropriately. The description of what speech is appropriate for self and other identification and for conducting one's life will allow them to describe communicative competence.

To describe the socially acceptable usage of speech, some sociolinguists stress the need for eliciting speech and contextual data. Hymes's ETHNOGRAPHY OF SPEAKING is perhaps the best known procedure for describing communicative competence so far. Since the task here is language description, sociolinguists seeking to describe communicative competence, not surprisingly, turned to descriptive linguistics for a model.*

The ethnography of speaking seeks to describe communicative competence by describing speech events (which occur in speech situations within a speech community) as series of speech acts composed of speech components. Speech compo-

---

*The reader is urged to note the parallels with descriptive linguistics as a model of language description. Data gathering is of primary importance. Where descriptivists analyze recurrent linguistic forms in different linguistic contexts or environments, sociolinguists in this approach look at recurrent messages in different social environments. However, note that while the data are speech, the object of description is actually communication.

nents are what a description of a speech act includes. The model suggests a mnemonic (that is, memory-assisting) device SPEAKING: (Setting, Participants, Ends (goals), Act (speech) sequences, Key (Tone), Instrumentalities (voice, gesture, etc.), Norms of interaction, Genres (song, speech, writing, etc.) Rules of speech may be formalized as well. The rules would be descriptions of what the components of speech events are, and what components in certain events are present or absent. (Hymes 1972:52–70) The rules are proposed to be formal statements of shifts in the components of speech.

Thus, the model is one of describing and isolating units of analysis at the various levels of language and society. The target of description is a speech community, not a language. Two principles are involved in defining a speech community: within it rules are shared for delivering and interpreting speech; within it rules are shared for interpreting at least one language or dialect (social or regional). (Hymes 1972:53)

Languages and dialects are likely to occur in the data to be described. If that is the case, then the linguist describes what speech varieties occur in which contexts (speech situations). The model may be schematized as follows:

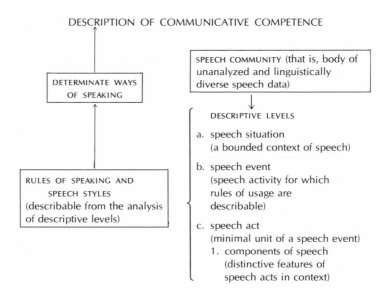

A simple example* would be:

1. SPEECH COMMUNITY: Western American academic community
   (for example, University of Washington)

2. SPEECH SITUATION: Interpersonal situations involving use of terms
   of address (for example, a departmental faculty-student lounge)

3. SPEECH EVENT: Use of address terms by an individual (for example,
   a college junior enters the lounge)

   a. SPEECH ACT: Use of a term for a particular individual (for example,
   the junior greets department chairperson)

   (POSSIBLE) COMPONENTS OF THE ACT

   (1) SETTING —faculty-student lounge
   (2) PARTICIPANTS— college junior and department chairperson
   (3) ENDS —junior who is a new major wishes to impress
   chairperson and behaves appropriately to that end
   (4) ACT SEQUENCE —junior uses correct form of address and
   appropriate content for the context (for example, *Hello,
   Professor X, I was intrigued by your lead article in the* Scholarly
   Blatt *this month.*)
   (5) KEY —serious, respectful
   (6) INSTRUMENTALITY —academese
   (7) NORMS OF INTERACTION —the junior speaks first, awaits a response,
   continues to use title etc.)
   (8) GENRE —dyadic conversation

4. RULES OF SPEAKING AND STYLE: For example:

   + [Higher + [15 years + [Identity → uses [Title + Last "Professor X"
   rank]   older]   set]   name]

5. (POSSIBLE) DETERMINATE WAYS OF SPEAKING: Abstraction and tentative
   generalization that encountering such features in an academic speech
   community a junior recently having declared a major would address
   his/her department chairperson as [Title + LN] (title plus last name).

6. COMMUNICATIVE COMPETENCE: It has been described here insofar as this
   example shows what an individual needed to know to behave
   appropriately in this culturally marked setting.

   *Expanded and elaborated from an example suggested by Ervin-Tripp
   1972:219

Thus, the model attempts to characterize a speech community by describing its levels (situations, events, acts) from
which rules of speech usage and speech styles may be extracted. The rules are envisioned as accounting for "ways of speak-

ing" in a speech community. The "ways of speaking" component of the model is an abstract notion at this point. The idea is that "the communicative behavior within a community is analyzable in terms of determinate ways of speaking, that the communicative competence of persons comprises in part a knowledge of determinate ways of speaking." (Hymes 1972: 58) Hymes claims this component necessarily needs to remain vague until more ethnographies of speaking are available. It is thought, however, that communicative competence is composed of rules of speaking and speech styles describable through the analysis of the levels of a speech community. By comparing descriptions of communities on this model, it may be possible to make statements regarding the nature of communicative behavior both in general and community specific.

Essentially, the method for describing communicative competence aims to bring in a sociolinguistic data base by providing a framework for the description and analysis of language use. Ethnographies of speaking are meant to be primarily concerned with providing observationally adequate descriptions of language use in speech communities definable through speech acts and events in community situations. The study of communicative competence by means of the ethnography of speaking attempts to account for all acceptable usages of speech in the various delimited speech situations comprising a speech community.

Eventually, it might be expected, the study of communicative competence may seek to account for the acquisition of communicative competence. But this would orient study from the proper use of the ethnography of speaking. We believe that

> . . . any proposal for a knowledge of the acquisition of communicative competence requires a theory of communication, just as for Chomsky knowledge of the acquisition of linguistic competence requires a theory of language. The competence/performance distinction made for language by Chomsky rests on competence defined as "the speaker-hearer's knowledge of his language" and performance defined as "the actual use of language in concrete situations." The communicative competence of the sociolinguist is defined . . . as "what a speaker needs to know to communicate effectively in culturally significant settings." Communicative competence, then, in

one sense is a type of performance concerned with how language is used (or performed) in context. One aim of descriptive sociolinguistics is to describe the various aspects or components of speech events as they occur (or are performed) in context. Another is to describe the acquisition of the ability or knowledge (competence) to communicate. (Eastman 1975: 116)

Moreover, ethnographers of speaking evision that:

. . . the next decade will see more and more ethnographic studies of speaking in schools, hospitals, and other institutions of contemporary culture in heterogeneous societies, toward the solution of practical social problems. If our work leads us to understand speaking in social life as adaptive and creative practice, and as a means for the creation of emergent structures, it is only appropriate that we endow the ethnography of speaking with a similar role. (Bauman and Sherzer 1974:12)

The types of study reviewed thus far toward describing communicative competence include studies of speech communities where more than one language or speech variety is spoken. Bilingual and multilingual studies are often encompassed here. Another type of study is that of social dialects centering on what the linguistic differences are that indicate such social conditions as social class and ethnic identity, religious affiliation, economic status, peer group status, privilege and seniority. Also studies are done of the use of oral literature in context (proverbs, tales, songs, myths) and of nonverbal communication in context (letter writing, written literature, sign language, and so on).

Most studies so far reveal that in a given speech community and its many speech situations speakers, who at some level share a common language, use differing rule systems. Thus, in a speech community speakers often miss each other's intentions which can cause problems in social interaction. If the rules for speech situations can be formulated such that the choices available for a speaker to make in order to speak appropriately in the situation are explicit, practical solutions to some problems of social interaction may be achieved. It also is possible to formulate rules to predict what speech items occur in sequence in certain types of discourse and what grammatical choices are realized in given contexts marking appropriate situational speech behavior. The sociolinguistic study of choices available to speakers with regard to style and decisions to use more than one language, and the phenomenon of changing what language or language variety is used in certain contexts by the same speakers as well as investigations as to what languages are appropriate for official and national use by particular countries in developing language policy — all represent new areas of investigation which can make contributions to education, government, and to society in general.

Many such studies are part of a broader sociology of language outside our main concern here yet fruitfully employing a number of notions from the ethnography of speaking. Language planning which is perhaps more a socioeconomic area of inquiry than language usage is developing through the combined efforts of social scientists, educators, and government leaders.

By looking at speech in culturally significant settings, the ethnography of speaking seeks to remedy a lack of concern in language description and linguistic theory with language usage. It is modeled after descriptive linguistics in its emphasis on the discovery and description of the structure of speech events in varying contexts throughout the world much as descriptive linguistics attempted to describe and discover the structure of speech in various languages throughout the world. It aims to show that speech events are distinguished from other verbal behavior in a describable rule-governed way.

> Constraints on performance structure in speech events are both paradigmatic, where they apply to selection among alternates [for example, terms of address], and syntagmatic, where they apply to the sequential order in which passages occur [for example, *Hello, Professor X, I was intrigued by your lead article in the* Scholarly Blatt rather than *Hello, Professor X, can ya loan me a fiver?*]. In this sense, rules of speaking seem akin to the grammatical rules applying to the production of sentences. (Gumperz 1975:xv)

Sociolinguists hold that there is a language structure above the sentence level. Their data include and describe

> . . . a level of structure that operates in the realm of discourse and is analytically separate from the grammar of individual

sentences. Communicative competence, that is, the ability to speak appropriately, implies a knowledge both of grammar and of rules of language usage. What Chomsky sees as human creativity — the speaker's freedom to create new sentences by innovative use of grammatical rules — is not simply a matter of free choice limited only by instrumental considerations of what the speaker wants to accomplish; it is also subject to social and ritual constraints. *(ibid.)*

In addition to the ethnography of speaking as an approach to the sociolinguistic study of communicative competence with its emphasis on describing the social variables influencing appropriate speech use, there is another approach to communicative competence stressing the linguistic variables which influence appropriate social behavior. This approach centers on the study of language structure and language change within various contexts in a speech community. The chief proponent of this type of sociolinguistic study is William Labov.

Because of the focus on linguistic rather than social variables, Labov is leery of the socio-prefix attached to this form of language description. Though moving beyond traditional levels of linguistic structure to encompass what is called discourse analysis, the type of study advocated by him is still language-based. According to Labov (1972:184),

The theoretical questions to be raised will also fall into the category of general linguistics. We will be concerned with the forms of linguistic rules, their combination into systems, the coexistence of several systems, and the evolution of these rules and systems with time. If there were no need to contrast this work with the study of language out of its social context, I would prefer to say that this was simply linguistics.

Before outlining Labov's method of sociolinguistic research as distinct from the ethnography of speaking, we should point out that there is still another approach to the study of speech usage, but which we are omitting since it is further removed from language description per se than are either of these approaches. This is the area known as the sociology of language which, though amenable to the ethnography of speaking as a model, is broader and more sociologically oriented. Influenced and fostered by Joshua Fishman, this field "deals with large-scale social factors, and their mutual interaction with languages and dialects." (Labov 1972:183)

In this area, one subfield—language planning—is emerging in which trained individuals with a knowledge of language description and of social science planning work in conjunction with government officials or group representatives to see that linguistic and cultural pride is developed and/or maintained within sociocultural entities in the interest of various goals such as nationalism, ethnicity, development, and so on.

Labov, however, has a linguistic goal in mind. Aware of generative grammar as a theory of language and Chomsky's lack of emphasis on the need for data to verify his theoretical claims, he predicates his position on the fact that a broader sample of data is available for theory testing when context is considered. Where the theory of generative grammar is evaluated as descriptively adequate according to internal evaluation measures, Labov believes that language "covariation and change in progress" can be studied and that language descriptions can be evaluated. Here again we encounter the distinction between linguistic theory and language description in Labov's claim that one can evaluate language descriptions. Disagreeing, Chomsky turned to devising an adequate formal theory of language. Yet, according to Labov (1972:202),

> The limitations placed upon the input data by Chomsky have led him to the conviction that the theory is underdetermined by the data (1966)—that there will always be many possible analyses for each body of data, and we will need internal evaluation measures to choose among them. We take the opposite view. Through the direct study of language in its social context, the amount of available data expands enormously, and offers us ways and means for deciding which of the many possible analyses is right. In our preliminary operations upon the initial data, considerations of simplicity will always find a place; but given the correct line of attack, it is possible to prove whether the simple hypothesis constructed is the correct one.

Labov feels strongly that it is important to study, describe and observe language directly. This view places him firmly in the descriptivist tradition. Furthermore, the direct study of language is broadened by describing language in its social context. Here the focus is the *language* in context, where to the ethnographers of speaking the focus is on describing the *context* for different varieties of language. Labov sees himself as interested in constructing a description to account for language in context. Much of his "new method" is concerned with how descriptions of the social use of language can use formalized rules operating on more abstract forms to understand why anyone says anything.

With a data-based orientation, Labov's proposal to describe linguistic covariation and change in context suggests that data be gathered in a number of spheres. Chief among them are that the linguist who traditionally relied on eliciting forms from an informant now records data through unsystematic observation (that is, speech of people unaware they are being observed); from the mass media (for example, speakers on interview programs or who call in to voice opinions); by asking informants to read passages (that is, to get their "formal" speech).

With such a sample of informants "styles," it is possible to describe individual speaker's varieties of speech as they covary with context. The data from varying social contexts are seen as providing the linguist with material to isolate "the basic vernacular." (Labov, 1972:223)

Labov believes that only by studying language in use can we describe the human ability to use rules of speech differently in different situations. Given his goal of describing language variation, this seems reasonable. In a passage where he seems to obscure the distinction between a theory of language and the description of speech variation, he makes this point in the context of the history of linguistics.

> The ability of human beings to accept, preserve and interpret rules with variable constraints is clearly an important aspect of their linguistic competence or *langue* [sic]. But no one is aware of this competence, and there are no intuitive judgments accessible to reveal it to us. Instead naive perception of our own and others' behavior is usually categorical, and only careful study of language in use will demonstrate the existence of this capacity to operate with variable rules. (1972: 226)

Interestingly enough, here is a a distinction stressed by Labovian sociolinguistics — namely, that between *categorical* and *variable* rules. Categorical rules apply regularly in a language; variable rules occur in some speakers (for whom percentages of likely applicability of the rule may be calculated), depending upon aspects of the context of the speaker and the speech event within a speech community. This distinction is important even though somewhat unfortunate because it creates confusion between (categorical) rules of linguistic competence (theory) and (variable) rules of speech (description). Gillian Sankoff, working along these lines, proposes "a quantitative paradigm for the study of communicative competence" in which this categorical/variable distinction is made explicit and resolves somewhat the theory/description confusion. Sankoff's model assumes that speech usage is statistically variable. In her view (1974:19), many sociolinguists now work "with situations in which rules appear to be more categorical than variable, situations of highly marked speech use including rituals, greetings, games, insults and the like." Such situations as we saw above for rules of address handled by the ethnography of speaking are amenable to being described by rules that are generally categorical. Sankoff believes, however, that quantitative techniques can be devised and applied to a speech data base to describe speech variability in more general, less stylized everyday speech situations.

Her proposal is that, with the speech community as the target of analysis, the sociolinguist needs to gather data "which adequately represents the speech performance of members of that community." (*ibid.*:21) To do so one must delineate the speech community, stratify the speech community, and decide on the number of informants and amount of material to be considered representative of the speech community.

The notion of *stratification* is distinctive in this model of sociolinguistics. Here, stratification means the assessment within the speech community of what "geographic, social and sociolinguistic dimensions of variation" exist. Thus, the focus here is to determine what speech is variable rather than what is categorical in a speech community as related to the stratified dimensions of variation within that community.

Labov (1972:237) defines a sociolinguistic variable as "one

which is correlated with some nonlinguistic variable of the social context: of the speaker, the addressee, the audience, the setting, etc." Furthermore, his approach (1972:237) stresses that:

> Some linguistic features (which we shall call *indicators*) show a regular distribution over socioeconomic, ethnic, or age groups, but are used by each individual in more or less the same way in any context. If the social context concerned can be ordered in some kind of hierarchy (like socioeconomic or age groups), these indicators can be said to be stratified.

In addition to *social stratification,* Labov sees a *stylistic stratification* operating in speech communities and he feels that this also needs to be described. Where *indicators* show social stratification, *markers* show stylistic stratification. Labov holds that both dimensions of a speech community (the social and stylistic) need to be quantified so that variability in actual speech can be measured against them.

Early studies from this approach to the study of speech use centered on phonological variables. One study dealt with the use of (r) in New York City by employees of three department stores—Saks, Macy's, and Klein's. The stores were judged as high-priced, middle-priced and low-priced respectively. The assumption was that customers in each store were socially stratified similarly—in other words, upper-class customers would shop in the high-priced store (Saks). Sales personnel were expected to reflect the dialects of their customers. In fact, it was assumed that salespeople would value their customers' dialect as prestigious. The anticipated result was that "salespeople in the highest-ranked store will have the highest values for (r), those in the middle-ranked store will have intermediate values of (r), and those in the lowest-ranked store will show the lowest values." (Reported in Labov 1972:45)

In the study, Labov examined four occurrences of (r) by employees in the three stores; that is, he elicited casual and emphatic usages of the phrase "fourth floor" in answer to the question, "Excuse me, what floor is this?" Where the (r) was plainly constricted, the value (r-1) was assigned. Where the (r) was omitted or replaced by schwa or a longer vowel (r-0) was the value. The results were that in Saks, 62 percent of the responses contained all or some (r-1), in Macy's 51 percent contained (r-1), and in Klein's only 20 percent of the responses had all or some (r-1). Thus, "as the hypothesis predicted, the groups are ranked by their differential use of (r-1) in the same order as their stratification by extralinguistic factors."

Since both casual and emphatic pronunciation was elicited, it was also possible to examine stylistic stratification in the same data. Labov discovered "extreme style-shifting" in the employees at Macy's while (r-1) was the norm at Saks and (r-0) at Klein's. Actually, since this study (1962), other studies of linguistic variation in various situations throughout New York City by Labov and in other cities by other researchers have led to a generalization that second highest status groups do styleshift more than groups at either extreme of the status scale. The style-shifting of mid-status groups is thought to be "associated with an extreme sensitivity to the norms of an exterior (usually prestigious) reference group" on the part of mid-status individuals. (1972:52 note 8)

Labov hopes that soon sociolinguistic studies of speech variation will transcend the analysis of phonological variables and analyze the variable use of more complex syntactic phenomena such as the use of relative clauses, negation, and the use of complements in sentences. (1972:247)

Sankoff (1974:25) notes that describing variation within a sociolinguistic model as suggested by Labov requires identifying "not only each instance of a particular variant, but also the number of instances in which it could have occurred, but did not." Her quantitative paradigm is an attempt to describe the formulation of grammatical rules for social and stylistic variations using such a probabilistic principle.

One of Labov's early studies used data from BEV (Black English vernacular) in contrast to SE (Standard English) and WNS₁ and WNS₂ (two White Non-Standard dialects). One variation was seen in the use of *negative concord* in differential ways in these dialects.

> In Black English when the verb is negated the indefinites *something, somebody,* and *some* become the negative indefinites *nothing, nobody,* and *none.* The rule is simple and elegant and quite common in the world's languages. This was the

rule which existed in earlier periods for all dialects of English. In Standard English, if the verb is negated the indefinites become *anything, anybody,* and *any.* If in the negative sentences in [Standard English] the forms *nothing, nobody* and *none* are used then the verb is not negated. (Fromkin and Rodman 1974:262)

Labov formulated a variable rule to account not only for these dialect differences but for variations occurring in some white nonstandard dialects. As a variable rule, it takes the most general form, – that is:

$$\text{NEG} - \text{X} - \begin{Bmatrix} \text{VERB} \\ \text{INDEF} \end{Bmatrix} \rightarrow$$

$$\quad 1 \qquad 2 \qquad 3 \qquad\qquad 1 \quad 2 \quad 1+3$$

The rule reads that in English dialects, verbs and indefinite determiners in the same clause are negated.

BEV *He don't know nothing.* (verb negated, indefinite determiner negated)

As a variable rule, it is accompanied by a table of conditions giving values (that is 0 = the rule never applies, X = the rule is variable, and 1 = the rule is obligatory or categorical) for each dialect. For example, for BEV, when the verb and indefinite determiner are not in the same clause the rule still operates so that sentences such as *It ain't no cat can't get in no coop* are possible in the BEV dialect but not in SE where the rule with a value of 0 applies that is, SE *There isn't any cat that can get in any coop.* In SE when the verb is negated in the first clause, it is not negated in the second and the indefinites in the environment of a negative verb are not negated. Consider also: SE *He doesn't know anything* (verb negated, indefinite determiner not negated), in contrast to the BEV example *He don't know nothing.*

   To speakers of all but the BEV dialect of English (including SE) the interpretation of the BEV *It ain't no cat can't get in no coop* is not its actual SE equivalent. Rather most speakers of non-Black dialects of English instead interpret the BEV sentence as *There is no cat that can't get into any coop.* As Labov states it comes as a surprise to discover from the context that [the speaker] was denying that cats were a problem, and that his meaning was "There isn't any cat that *can* get into any coop."

The types of study carried out by Labovian sociolinguists focus on describing the differences among the speech, writing, and gesture varieties within their contexts of use so that linguistic features are correlated with factors such as social class differences, ethnic differences, sex differences, geographical location, and peer group status. This differs markedly with studies by ethnographers of speaking who center on describing phenomena such as bilingualism, multilingualism, and use of different speech varieties in different situations. Where the ethnographer of speaking wishes to describe language as a part of culture, the sociolinguist focusing on speech variability seeks understanding of the "mechanism of linguistic change" through study of the social factors motivating linguistic evolution.

Labov (1972:326) holds that linguistic variability studies will lead to an understanding of language change because language change operates in a social milieu. Not all scholars who deal with linguistic change agree that social factors are as important as Labov feels them to be. However, he illustrates his particular view by looking at sound change as occurring in the following fashion. Change is first observed in a particular subgroup. It spreads to neighboring groups, carrying with it prestige and social value from the originating group. Then, the change becomes generalized in the originating group. New social groups move into the area of the originating group and reinterpret the change. "As the original change acquires greater complexity, scope, and range, it comes to acquire more systematic social value, and is restrained or corrected in formal speech (a marker). Eventually, it may be labelled as a *stereotype,* discussed and remarked by everyone." (1973:326) Once stereotyped, the change if high in prestige value may be adopted by the dominant dialect "at the expense of the older form." If the change has negative prestige, it may "be stigmatized, corrected, and even extinguished." (*ibid.*)

Animal Communication

As sociolinguistics has broadened the scope of language description to include analyzing speech varieties and dialects in their contexts of use, animal communication, another current research field, aims to describe languages by focusing on gesture and symbol manipulation as indicators of linguistic ability. As with sociolinguistics, the object of description becomes in this case more communication than speech. As Fromkin and Rodman (1974:174) put it:

> If language is viewed only as a system of communication, then obviously many species communicate . . . To understand human language one needs to see what, if anything, is special and unique in language. If we find that there are no such special properties then we will have to conclude that language, as we have been discussing it, is not, as claimed, uniquely human.

Current interest and research in animal communication can be credited to some impressive results obtained by researchers who describe ability to communicate with chimpanzees. Researchers describe the communicative performance of animals such as chimpanzees based on observations. Most work in this area of language description is done by experimental psychologists interested in language. Such people may be broadly defined as psycholinguists. They study language behavior, how children acquire language and how language is encoded, decoded, produced, and understood. Animal communication as language description interprets language as communication; therefore, it is the study of how language is encoded, decoded, produced, and understood by animals as compared to humans.

To describe a language as a system of communication also broadens the scope of the task in another direction — toward the description and analysis of signs as units of a communicational or signaling system. This field, known as SEMIOTICS, is an outgrowth of structural linguistics.

The approach here originated with de Saussure's methods and theories. In fact, de Saussure urged development of the approach in order to corroborate the distinction he proposed between speech *(parole)* and language as a structural system *(langue)*. De Saussure, writing at the beginning of this century, held that a linguistic *sign* which "unites, not a thing and a name, but a concept and a sound image" (1916, p. 66 of 1959 English translation) could be expanded to include communication *signs*. Moreover,

> Language is a system of signs that express ideas, and is therefore comparable to a system of writing, the alphabet of deaf-mutes, symbolic rites, polite formulas, military signals etc . . . *A science that studies the life of signs within society* is conceivable; it would be a part of social psychology and consequently of general psychology: I shall call it semiology [or semiotics] (from Greek sēmeion "sign"). Semiology would show what constitutes signs, what laws govern them. Since the science does not yet exist, no one can say what it would be; but it has a right to existence, a place staked out in advance. Linguistics is only a part of the general science of semiology; the laws discovered by semiology will be applicable to linguistics, and the latter will circumscribe a well-defined area within the mass of anthropological facts. *(ibid)*

Within a communicational approach to language, an interest developed in describing the differences between human language and any nonhuman communicative system.

According to Charles Hockett (1958:574–80), a structural linguist, human languages have a set of seven properties which is nonexistent in nonhuman communication: *duality*—having both phonological and grammatical systems; *productivity*—having utterances never heard before; *arbitrariness*—not correlating a thing with its label; *interchangeability*—speaking as well as hearing; *specialization; displacement*—containing "antecedents and consequences" removed "from the time and place of transmission"; *cultural transmission*.

Ten years later, he modified the features and indicated that not all are necessary to delimit human from nonhuman communication (cf. Altmann 1968). Nevertheless, considerable research centers on testing the linguistic behavior of apes against Hockett's 1958 set of properties. Recent research attempting to teach chimpanzees to communicate seems to indicate that if such features define human language, chimpanzees have languages too.

Recently researchers have tried to teach chimpanzees American Sign Language (Ameslan) as a means of communication. In other words, they have tried to teach them to manipulate gestural "signs." Working with three chimps, Washoe, Lucy, and Ally, psychologist Roger Fouts found that chimps have the same set of language properties as humans. (Linden 1974:149ff) Research has begun to show that certain of the properties have been described based on observations of the chimpanzees who "learned" Ameslan. Fouts is currently testing the chimpanzees for the set of human language design features in their use of Ameslan among themselves. (Linden 1974:150) Duality, arbitrariness, and specialization are not included in tests because he believes they have been already sufficiently demonstrated. The fact that the chimps use Ameslan and that the gestures are not derivable from their referents indicates the presence of the duality and arbitrariness features. Beatrice and Allen Gardner, researchers with whom Fouts worked originally, demonstrated the feature of specialization through their observations of Washoe appropriately using Ameslan. David Premack, another researcher, working with the chimp, Sarah, also showed the presence of the three features excluded by Fouts.

To illustrate this, we will consider briefly David Premack's research with Sarah. Where other researchers used Ameslan, Premack used a graphic communication system in a "synthetic language of tokens." (Linden 1974:172) Sarah's language showed a number of the design features of human language.

> Like Ameslan, Premack's medium has duality—a grammar and the equivalent of phonemes. The tokens satisfy the criterion of arbitrariness because Premack has purposefully made them arbitrary. The fact that token messages educe appropriate behavior from Sarah indicates that the language has specialization. (Linden 1974:174)

Premack's work, like Fouts's, also has produced evidence for the other design features in Hockett's list of necessary features of speech. Researchers today working with chimps using either

Ameslan or graphic symbols focus on demonstrating that the sign "language" or symbol manipulation "language" of chimpanzees contain the features of human "language."

For our purposes, we will outline Fouts's current research plans for observing a colony of Ameslan-using chimps. To demonstrate the other four features of human language, his procedure involves *interchangeability* — observing chimpanzees communicate with each other and describing the communication; *cultural transmission* — observing chimps who "know" a gesture (that the others don't know) "teach" the others to use it appropriately, as well as noting whether or not mother chimps "teach" their infants Ameslan; *productivity* — introducing new objects to the chimpanzees to see if they introduce new signs for them and use the signs; and *displacement* — observing whether or not chimps can communicate "about events displaced in time and space from the immediate environment." (Linden, 1974:156)

Displacement is the most controversial language feature regarding human versus animal communication. It is what allows humans to recall the past and speculate about the future. Nonhumans generally lack this ability because they can respond only instantly to stimuli. In fact, given the behaviorist nature of animal communication research, it is difficult to find results which show any displacement feature in animal communication. However, some evidence for displacement is attributed to the following result (Linden 1974:53–54):

> One day after several failed attempts to teach her "no," the Gardners told Washoe that there was a big dog outside that wanted to eat her. A little later they asked her if she wanted to go out. Washoe said "no." The stimulus that caused Washoe to say "no" was only her memory that earlier she had been told that there was a big dog out there — an event not concurrent with the act of communication.

Like tagmemics, the work by Fouts, Premack, and the Gardners with the chimps Washoe, Sarah, and Ally is empirically based and behavioristic. The "language" of the chimps is taught to them by humans who provide a *stimulus* to the chimps who are *rewarded* when they make an appropriate *response.* If Fouts's colony of chimps demonstrate the behaviors he hoped to observe and describe, it might be possible to show that what the chimps have acquired in their use of Ameslan is something more than a conditioned response to gestural stimuli.

When Washoe reportedly said "no" to a question which would have received a "yes" had she not recalled prior information, then she initiated the behavior herself. This "creative" use of Ameslan is not possible as a behaviorist result but seems to suggest the acquisition by Washoe of "some developing gestalt *displaced* from the act of communication" rather than her having been "programmed to perform a complex gestural dance." (Linden 1974:238)

Is the description of chimpanzees using Ameslan or manipulating tokens in a "meaningful" way really *language* description?

Fromkin and Rodman (1974:183) claim that despite Washoe and Sarah, "the more animal communication systems we examine, the more sure we become that language is a human characteristic." They make this claim based on the ideas that (1) chimpanzees must be taught language, (2) chimpanzees do not initiate conversations, and (3) chimpanzees respond *because* of rewards.

Furthermore,

> If language is defined merely as a system of communication, then language is not unique to man. There are, however, certain characteristics of human language which are not found in the communication systems of any other species. A basic property of human language is its creative aspect — a speaker's ability to string together *discrete units* to form an *infinite* set of "well-formed" novel sentences. Also, children need not be taught language in any controlled way; they require only linguistic input to enable them to form their own grammar.
>
> The fact that deaf children learn language shows that the ability to hear or produce sounds is not a necessary prerequisite for language learning. And the ability to "imitate" the sounds of human language is not a sufficient basis for the learning of language, since "talking" birds imitate sounds but can neither segment these sounds into smaller units not understand what they are imitating.

Birds, bees, crabs, wolves, dolphins, chimpanzees, and most other animals communicate in some way. Limited information is imparted, and emotions such as fear, and warnings, are emitted. But the communication systems are fixed and limited. They are *stimulus-bound*. This is not so of human language. Experiments to teach animals more complicated language systems have historically failed. Recently, however, some chimps have demonstrated an ability to master some subset of a human language. It is possible that the higher primates have the limited ability to be taught *some* complex rules. To date, however, language still seems to be unique to man. (Fromkin and Rodman 1974:188)

It must be remembered here that the behaviorist experiments conducted with chimpanzees are generally testing for the presence of language defined according to a set of design features proposed by Hockett for defining language as speech. Yet, the work is done in a broader communicational framework where the features are attributed to gestural and symbol manipulative features. For language description, the animal behaviorist and ethological researchers need to analyze the content in gestures and symbols having once taught them. This is difficult in any approach to language description (as speech or as communicational content *and* expression). It also may be impossible with animal "language" because speech (gestural, using tokens) only occurs between different species (apes and humans)!

The rationalists consider this not only impossible but not worth pursuing. In their view, animals "have" no language if it is taught to them by humans and humans are the only beings with which the taught animals can communicate. The behaviorists, however, can place such broadened communicational research into a we-are-all-part-of-nature scheme. As Linden (1974:287) notes:

While scientists are talking to chimps, ordinary people have for a few years been talking with their plants. Here, the idea is that the visceral elements of communication have meaning not just across phyla, an idea that revitalizes organisms almost universally perceived to be "unsacrosanct raw material." People are increasingly disavowing synthetic foods and drugs and applauding the virtues of natural foods and cures. Among the young there is an undercurrent pantheistic spirit reflected in the growth of the conservation movement, the repopulation of rural areas and a Dionysian celebration of nature and the senses.

The point is not to suggest the validity of these various phenomena, but to suggest that they are expressive of a shared intuition of the inadequacy of the rational world and are also expressive of the shared need to reestablish communication with nature.

Although most work assumes a validity to Hockett's design features of speech as definitional for language as communication, it is not at all clear that Hockett meant this to be. Some scholars believe that what Washoe does at best is exhibit quasi-linguistic behavior — for the description of Washoe's use of Ameslan "is based on disparate descriptive features of human languages, taken at random, and without previous theoretical justification of the defining criteria assigned to human language." (Mounin 1976:3)

If Fouts's chimpanzees fail to teach Ameslan to their offspring, would this mean they have no language or that Ameslan is not salient for chimpanzee cultural transmission? A number of such questions come to mind when attempting to describe and analyze the possibility of and evidence for animal communication.

To one scientist who believes that in chimpanzees "there is no language properly speaking" (Mounin 1976:2), the research underway is nonetheless valid in a sphere of language description beyond the analysis of speech. Where tagmemics is seen as part of a description of human behavior and stratificational grammar is an effort to describe human communication, studies of animal communication should proceed because primatologists, ethologists, and anthropologists will appreciate the wealth and quality of the data and descriptions as well as the importance of the anthropological questions posed.

Bellugi and Klima (1973:106) claim that human language is distinctly different from animal communication in terms of its productivity because human language can "produce indefinitely many sentences never heard before, whose meanings can be understood as precisely by anyone else who shares the language." Moreover, the pairing of *productivity* and interpretability which a shared system of grammar provides is what makes human language such a versatile communication system,

> so versatile that not only can we express things that are outside of our immediate experience, we can even express the inconceivable. Not only can we relate past events and predict future ones, not only can we lie and indeed create whole fictitious worlds, but we can even communicate our more irrational fantasies. (*ibid.*)

Research in Linguistic Theory

Today research in linguistic theory focuses on developing formal models to account for language as a cognitive structure which exists in humans alongside other cognitive structures. The work may be seen in two approaches: the work of various TG linguists on the components of a linguistic theory; the work on language as an aspect of developing models of artificial intelligence and work on language acquisition from the point of view of language as a cognitive structure.

Generative Phonology and Linguistic Theory

As discussed in Chapter Four, Chomsky's work has had a great impact on linguistic theory. Current debates seem to focus on the nature of the syntactic and semantic components of a *Theory of Language* as a cognitive structure. All TG theorists agree that a formal theory of language may be conceived of as a formal model of the process of the acquisition of linguistic knowledge and they also all agree that there is a phonological component. Since there is considerable agreement as to the nature of a rule-governed phonology as part of a theory of language, it will be our intent here to discuss what linguistic theorists, especially generative phonologists, do. Generative phonologists see their work as having implications for the explanation of "perceptual processes and the conditions under which knowledge of a language (and, presumably, knowledge of other sorts) can be acquired." (Chomsky and Halle 1968:vii) Generative phonology is available for systematic review in at least one form—the theory presented by Noam Chomsky and Morris Halle in *The Sound Pattern of English* (1968).

This work is a descriptive study of English phonology, based on descriptions done in earlier grammars and also on descriptions by the authors themselves of their own speech. As Chomsky and Halle (1968:viii) explain it:

> We are not . . . concerned exclusively or even primarily with the facts of English as such. We are interested in these facts for the light they shed on linguistic theory (on what, in an earlier period, would have been called "universal grammar") and for what they suggest about the nature of mental processes in general.

Further, what researchers present as a descriptive study of English phonology is likely to be inaccurate and "require substantial revision as research progresses." (*ibid.*:ix) This approach is the converse of the descriptive studies done as language description.

> One of the best reasons for presenting a theory of a particular language in the precise form of a generative grammar, or for presenting a hypothesis concerning general linguistic theory in very explicit terms, is that only such precise and explicit formulation can lead to the discovery of serious inadequacies and to an understanding of how they can be remedied. In contrast, a system of transcription or terminology, a list of examples, or a rearrangement of the data in a corpus is not "refutable" by evidence (apart from inadvertence—errors that are on the level of proofreading mistakes). It is for just this reason that such exercises are of very limited interest for *linguistics as a field of rational inquiry.* (emphasis mine) (*ibid.*:ix.).

What the generative phonologist does is propose formal devices to describe phonology. The formal devices are considered part of *the* theory of language. When formal devices are proposed to account for the sound system of a particular language (for example, English), the devices are considered to be not *the* theory of phonology in all languages but the "part of the theory of language underlying the description of English" presented by the researchers (1968:330) as a result of their investigation.

The analysis of the sound structure of a particular language intended as part of generative phonological theory consists of:
1. A system of rules which are derivative of rewrite rules which we saw earlier as used in syntax. The rules are of the form:

$$A \rightarrow B \ / \ X \underline{\hspace{2em}} Y]_V$$

which "states that an element of type A is rewritten [or actualized] as a corresponding element of the type B when A appears in the context X _____ Y (that is with X to its left and Y to its right) and when the item in question is a verb, i.e., is dominated by V or, equivalently, is bracketed by $[_V]_V$." (1968:14)
2. The rules relate surface structures to phonetic representations. That is, the rules would relate (a) to (b) below. The symbol + represents a formative boundary.

(a)

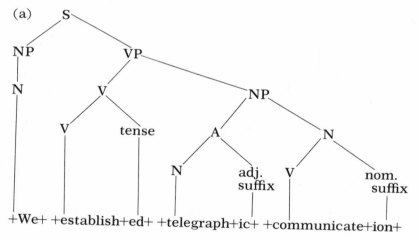

+We+ +establish+ed+ +telegraph+ic+ +communicate+ion+

(b) wīy + əstǽblɪšt + tèləgrǽfɪk + kəmyùwnəkéyšən
(modified from Chomsky and Halle 1968:8–14)

The surface structure of (a) (that is, the final line of the derivation) may more conveniently be represented by labeled bracketing. In other words, $[_S [_{NP} [_N + WE+]_N]_{NP} [_{VP} [_V [_V +ESTAB\text{-}LISH+]_V +PAST+]_V [_{NP} [_A [_N +TELEGRAPH+]_N +IC+]_A [_N [_V +COMMUNICATE+]_V +ION+]_N]_{NP}]_{VP}]_S$.

3. Both surface structures and phonetic representations are depicted as feature matrices:

> . . . phonetic representation [that is, (b) above] . . . is actually a
> feature matrix in which the rows correspond to a restricted set
> of universal phonetic categories or features (voicing, nasality,
> etc.) and the columns to successive segments . . . each forma-
> tive of the surface structure [i.e. (a) above] can also be repre-
> sented as a feature matrix interpreted in a rather similar way,
> with rows corresponding to the universal phonetic and gram-
> matical categories. The formative structure is much more ab-
> stract, however; its relation to the speech signal is not as direct
> as that of phonetic representation. (1968:14)

4. "The rules of the phonological component have a fixed form and a specific organization, . . . apply in a fixed manner determined by the labeled bracketing of the surface structure, and . . . meet various additional conditions depending on their formal relations." (*ibid.*)

The theory of language claims that in its phonological component (1) rewrite rules are used, (2) phonetic representations are related to surface structures, (3) phonetic representations and surface structures are represented by feature matrices, and (4) rules have a fixed form, apply in a fixed manner, and are subject to conditions imposed by their formal relations with each other. On the basis of these assumptions, formal devices are proposed to account for the relationship of phonetic representations to surface structures. Thus, the phonological component of a TG grammar as a theory of language is a formal model in its own right. Theorists working on the syntactic and semantic components are likewise guided by assumptions of a similar nature but specific to the structures within them to be related. The formal devices of each component constitute the grammar and hence a theory of language.

Once the formal devices for relating phonetic representations and surface structures are proposed they must meet "several conditions of adequacy" and serve various functions. These conditions and functions imposed on the formal devices

> . . . must, moreover, permit us to formulate general statements about the language which are true and significant, and must provide a basis for distinguishing these from other generalizations which are false, or which are true but not significant. *Thus if our analysis is correct, the rules . . . represent true and significant generalizations: they characterize the native speaker's competence, his idealized ability to produce and understand an unlimited number of sentences.* (emphasis mine) (Chomsky and Halle 1968:330)

Theoretical linguistic research involves proposing and evaluating formal devices based on the stated assumptions of the theory in order to make significant generalizations about language.

Chomsky expresses the empirical reality to which TG theory ultimately relates as *the* fundamental problem of the linguist. The linguist aims

> to account for the child's construction of a grammar and to determine what preconditions on the form of language make it possible. Our approach to this problem is two-pronged. First, we develop a system of formal devices for expressing rules and a set of general conditions on how these rules are organized and how they apply. We postulate that only grammars meeting these conditions are "entertained as hypotheses" by the child who must acquire knowledge of a language. Secondly, we determine a procedure of evaluation that selects the highest valued of a set of hypotheses of the appropriate form, each of which meets a condition of compatibility with the primary linguistic data . . . . . we face the empirical problem of selecting a set of formal devices and an evaluation procedure which jointly meet the empirical condition that the highest valued grammar of the appropriate form, is, in fact, the one selected by the child on the basis of primary linguistic data. (1968:331)

Thus, linguistics as a theory of language acquisition is unabashedly abstract. Linguists, then, are striving to develop a formal theory that will meet conditions of internal consistency, exhaustiveness, and simplicity. It is linguistics as a theory of language, then, which followed the appeals of the structuralists (such as Harris and Hjelmslev) to aim for a formal theory. Yet, the nature of the theory is *generative*, not structuralist. The process of understanding sentences is seen as language acquisition in the TG model. As such, language acquisition ultimately is not an instantaneous process although Chomsky (1968:31) admits much theoretical research makes it seem that way.

> We have been describing acquisition of language as if it were an instantaneous process. Obviously, this is not true. A more realistic model of language acquisition would consider the order in which primary linguistic data are used by the child and the effects of preliminary "hypotheses" developed in the earlier stages of learning in the interpretation of new, often more complex data. To us, it appears that this more realistic study is much too complex to be undertaken in any meaningful way today and that it will be far more fruitful to investigate in detail, as a first approximation, the idealized model . . ., leaving refinements to a time when this idealization is better understood.

Psycholinguistics: Child Language Acquisition and Artificial Intelligence

Psycholinguistics involves behavioral studies of language (such as the research done on chimpanzee versus human language), studies of how children acquire language, and studies of how language is encoded, decoded, produced and understood. Studies of child language and of artificial intelligence are theoretical linguistically in that they are attempts to know how a "correct" model of linguistic competence is used.

CHILD LANGUAGE ACQUISITION

Most studies made under this rubric with an aim to connect theory and the acquisition process in the child are known as DEVELOPMENTAL PSYCHOLINGUISTICS. Fromkin and Rodman (1976:307) distinguish theoretical linguistics and psycholinguistics this way:

The study of *what* children learn—the grammar—is the study of linguistic competence. The study of *how* children acquire this knowledge and how we use language to speak and understand is the study of linguistic performance (or language BEHAVIOR). This area of linguistics is called PSYCHOLINGUISTICS, since it deals with the psychological, behavioral aspects of language.

Developmental psycholinguists observe the development of language in children (performance) as a reflection of their innate capacity for language (competence). They believe that children are born with competence which "takes the form of linguistic universals" (Fraser 1966 re. McNeil 1966 in Lyons and Wales [eds.] 1966:116), which consist of "the basic notions in a Chomskian transformational grammar." In other words, metaphorically speaking, a child is now born with a copy of *Aspects of the Theory of Syntax* tucked away somewhere inside." (*ibid.*)

Prior to this theory-related approach to the study of language acquisition in children, the prevailing view was couched in learning theory. According to Fraser (1966:115):

Language, it was felt, was THE instance of a complex learned skill, with a minimum of specific biological mechanisms being necessary for learning to take place. It would have been conceded that man needed control over the motor mechanisms of speech and that he required some sort of general intellectual capacity to acquire language; but apart from those, language was well and truly a learned achievement. As Carroll (1964) has put it: "Human language . . . is always learned. Each child must learn his language from scratch . . ." And, starting from scratch, a child learned language by means of a mixture of imitation, selective reinforcement and generalization.

Today, learning has been deemphasized somewhat in the light of evidence from linguistic theory. Developmental psychologist Roger Brown (1973:58) sees the study of child language acquisition to be the study of knowledge "concerning grammar and the meanings coded by grammar," not how "the child's mind in fact processes sentences in speaking and understanding."

Developmental psychologists consider child language acquisition to occur in approximately five stages on a continuum with developments characterizing each stage often interrelating with other stages. Brown's stages are:

1. Semantic roles and syntactic relations are related in a simple sentence.

2. Grammatical morphemes and the modulation of meaning occur in a simple sentence.

3. Modalities are added to expand the simple sentence.

4. Sentences are embedded one within another.

5. Simple sentences and propositional relations are coordinated.

We will use *Mr. Smith cut the rope with a knife* to show what is added through the stages.

Stage One: *Mr. Smith cut the rope with a knife.*
The three NPs (*Mr. Smith, the rope, a knife*) have different semantic roles and syntactic functions in the sentence (that is, subject, object, and agent respectively).

Stage Two: *Mr. Smith would've cut the ropes with the knives.*
At this stage the basic semantic roles and the syntactic rules are further "modulated" (that is, inflected for plural, tense, aspect, degrees of reference, prepositions etc.).

Stage Three: *Shouldn't Mr. Smith have cut the ropes with the knife?*
Here, sentences can be "transformed" whole into other modalities (for example, yes-no questions, imperatives, general interrogatives and negatives are produced).

Stage Four: *I wish that Mr. Smith who brought the knife would not have cut the ropes with it.*

Stage Five: *Mr. Smith and the knife cut the rope.*
Brown (1973:32) suggests that these stages "constitute the core of English Sentence construction and, with some allowance for variation in syntax and meaning, of language generally."

There is debate among scholars of language acquisition as to whether or not grammatical patterns are inherited. Most TG linguists argue that language has an inherited and specific capacity. For example, Bolinger (1975:277) believes that,

> The grammar of a language is held to contain an extremely elaborate abstract system of rules. If the child is too young to form such rules, then he must inherit them in some form or other. And to counter the opposing argument that even with feeble abstracting powers the child still might build the rules from observation, it is pointed out that what he hears is too defective to serve as a model.

Brown (1973 in Miller 1973:116) is not as committed to the innateness position. He contends that more evidence of many types is needed to show that the development of language in children takes a universal course. If such evidence is available,

> It may mean, in the first place, that all the languages of the world have certain structural features in common, that there is a universal definition of language. In fact this much is already established by descriptive and theoretical linguistics. A universal order of development may furthermore mean that the brain of our species is programmed to operate in quite definite ways upon any materials that manifest the properties of language: that language materials set off programs of analysis which discover in these materials those structural properties that are not universal, the rules that are local and variable; and that rules of various kinds are sought in a fixed order.

As a result of developmental studies of language acquisition, interest has also ranged to the biological and neurological foundations of language. Most linguists feel that language is ultimately related to cognition and perception. If so, then an understanding of the acquisition process would be aided by knowledge of the nature of cognition and perception and of the development and workings of the brain. There is general agreement among scholars in linguistics that research needs to be done on what neurological aspects are involved in the human ability to acquire and use language. Available research on language and the brain shows that the left side of the brain is involved in language for right-handed people and vice versa. The brain, unlike the rest of the nervous system, is lateralized and asymmetrical rather than symmetrical. In other words, where generally humans (and many other animals) have "two of everything" (eyes, legs, arms) and "what exists on the left exists on the right," with the human brain the situation differs in that, though divided into left and right hemispheres, the brain has "one of everything" distributed in different hemispheres. Usually language is a function of the left side of the brain. Further research indicates that the specialization for language is for language alone and not for all human sound. Laughing, for example, is generally perceived and interpreted in the right hemisphere.

> This asymmetry of the human brain is one of man's unique characteristics. It has been argued that this "division of labor" explains man's intellectual and language abilities. In all other animals each side of the brain is equally responsible for all "mental activities." But in man each side has developed its own "talents" and this specialization may permit increased mental powers, one of which, perhaps the most important, is the ability to learn language. (Fromkin and Rodman 1974: 315)

Most specialists in this type of research feel that lateralization of the brain in terms of its functions is involved in the acquisition of language by children. In fact, it seems to be the case that when the brain is fully developed (lateralized) in children (at approximately four or five years of age) the acquisition of language is complete. What is not known is whether the linguistic ability that seems to develop in a way parallel to brain lateralization is a related phenomenon. Moreover, it is not known how the linguistic ability involved in language acquisition relates to other cognitive abilities.

Research on the brain as it develops and on language acquisition developmentally, insofar as parallels occur, may indicate that the facts of language acquisition may be universal but not necessarily innate. The view which counters the innateness hypothesis is that language acquisition in part involves *sensorimotor* intelligence—that is, that it involves a physical response to external stimuli. For example, psychologist Jean Piaget "has shown that sensorimotor intelligence develops out of the infants' commerce with objects and persons during the first 18–24 months of life." (Brown 1973:198)

Perhaps future research will reveal that language acquisition can only be understood as part of general cognitive ability. McNeil (1966:115) has suggested that it would be fruitful to find out if Piaget's views of sensorimotor development and his other proposed stages of language acquisition

> could be interpreted as the unfolding of a transformational system . . . without an analysis of the system acquired in cognitive development that is comparable to the linguistic analysis of syntax, a comparison of the speed of cognitive and linguistic development is simply not possible. That cognitive development is apparently complete by the age of four, may only mean that the acquisition of a system of general knowledge is three times as complex as the acquisition of English.

However, in terms of his theory, Chomsky does not feel that neurological factors of cognition present any real challenge to the idea of language acquisition as an example of a cognitive structure acquired through an innate ability. His view (1975: 138) is that

> . . . humans are innately endowed with a system of intellectual organization, call it the "initial state" of the mind. Through interaction with the environment and maturational processes, the mind passes through a sequence of states in which cognitive structures are represented. In the case of language it is fairly obvious that rapid and extensive changes take place during an early period of life, and a "steady state" is achieved which then undergoes only minor modifications. Abstracting away from the latter, we can refer to this steady state as the "final state" of the mind, in which knowledge of language is somehow represented. We can construct hypotheses concerning the initial and final state and can proceed to validate, or reject, or sharpen these hypotheses by methods of inquiry that are familiar. We might proceed, in principle, to explore the physical realizations of the initial and final states and the processes involved in the changes of state that take place.

The field of child language acquisition is one which relies on the three-pronged research effort now underway among developmental psychologists seeking to characterize the stages at which children acquire various aspects of linguistic perfor- mance ability, among theoretical linguists seeking to charac- terize the nature of the cognitive structure of knowledge un- derlying performance, and among the new breed of neuro- linguists seeking to characterize the relationship of cognitive structures in general to the working and development of the brain.

ARTIFICIAL INTELLIGENCE

In Chapter Two we saw that automata theory and the advent of digital computers provided the wherewithal to begin formal- izing a theory of linguistic structure and that this led to the development of TG grammar. With the computer age came machines that linguists could use as tools. We saw earlier that original MT efforts were sparked by machine advances and that these efforts employed models of grammatical description in an attempt to translate automatically texts from one lan- guage to another. These endeavors took advantage of the stor- age capacity of computers and applied analytical discovery procedures from various approaches to language description to attempt to meet this goal. However, it became clear that, with- out a theory for understanding language, trying to get comput- ers to do what requires human intelligence produced superfi- cial results and in the long run proved to be unproductive.

Since the 1950s and early 1960s progress has been made in arriving at a theory of "understanding" sentences in theoreti- cal linguistics. Concomitantly work has begun anew in re- search involving computers and language. The purpose of this research on language is part of a larger effort aimed at general understanding or intelligence. The research is based on a num- ber of assumptions centering on a concept of ARTIFICIALITY.

The artificial may be differentiated from the natural as fol- lows:
1. It is synthesized by man.
2. It may "imitate appearances in natural things" while lack- ing their reality.

3. It is characterizable in terms of "functions, goals, adaptations."

4. It is discussed both as how it is and how it ought to be. (after Simon 1969:5–6)

Natural-language processing in artificial intelligence studies aims to produce a normative model for natural language as part of human intelligence or cognition. Actually, artificial intelligence (henceforth, AI) is often synonymous with the term *simulation of cognitive processes.*

Michie (1974:103), an AI researcher, summed up the state of the field *vis-à-vis* computer analysis of language thusly:

> In the 1950s and 1960s, millions of dollars were spent in the United States on research-and-development projects aimed at this. The techniques of machines breaking up texts grammatically and looking up meanings in a computer dictionary proved too shallow to crack the machine translation problem unaided. Fundamental progress had to wait for the development of an adequate theory of what is involved in "understanding" a passage of English-language text. The needed theory is only just beginning to emerge. The syntactic and semantic problems presented by natural language are at present under study . . . But this is only one of many areas in which we can attempt to achieve "computer understanding."

Natural-language processing is the area of concern that we will discuss here as an aspect of AI which makes use of advances in theoretical linguistics.* The processing of natural language, like the work on TG theory, involves the notion of *understanding* as a goal. Where TG theory aims to make the process of understanding sentences explicit, AI researchers seek to construct programs for understanding natural language. Where, to the theoretical linguist, sentences are the object of theory application, in AI studies of natural language, the concept of language is a communicational one. Programs underway are being fashioned so they might literally understand communication in natural languages.

In a sense, AI research on language hopes to build linguistic

---

*Most of the research being done today is in the United States (Stanford, MIT, Bolt, Berenek and Newman, Inc.) and in Scotland (Edinburgh University).

competence into a machine such that the machine will be able to understand and respond to natural language. That is, it is hoped that programs may be written so that machines may engage in dialog with humans. In an understatement, Feigenbaum and Feldman (1963:8) put the situation this way: "...one would like to be able to engage in a dialog with a computer—a dialog in which the computer will hold up its end of the conversation adaptively, intelligently . . . ." In an admittedly simplified discussion here we will characterize the type of questions being asked and assumptions being operated on by researchers working on natural-language processing. Our concern will be mainly with research which relates to language defined as understanding and/or cognition rather than with particular models and descriptions of "real" linguistic data.

In fact, in artificial intelligence, research toward the development of natural language processors are of two types: the one more theoretical and aimed at programing comprehension, the other more applied and aimed at translation and analysis.

> Efforts to develop natural language processors fall between artificial intelligence and information retrieval. There is no hard and fast rule to distinguish when a particular application is in one field or the other. We can distinguish some end points. Programs that search for a particular sequence of letters in a text, but do nothing more than record the occurrence or nonoccurrence of the sequence, although very useful in indexing and abstracting, are seldom considered artificial intelligence examples. Programs that compose complex and varied replies to a user, even though those replies are keyed by single words in the input stream, are in the artificial intelligence field. (Hunt 1975:16)

In efforts to write programs to process natural languages there are a number of central concerns. One central concern is the realization that it is necessary to discover just how to understand a topic or problem.

One approach to this problem is to make use of robots. AI researchers in Edinburgh feel that robots may be used to develop a number of theories of "computer understanding" of the real world. The theories can be tested by the robots themselves.

The AI researchers believe that if robots can be made to *understand* how to find, fetch, build, and tidy, they can be programed to carry out those operations. Without this understanding of operations built in, no program can be written to execute the tasks.

Michie (1974:104–5) provides an example of a man-machine dialogue which involved a number of programs which interlock in various places, using a dictionary of 200 English words. The resulting dialog used two-and-a-half-million units of information as the computer memory!

MAN: *Will you please stack up both of the red blocks and either a green cube or a pyramid?*

MACHINE: OK.

MAN: *Which cube is sitting on the table?*

MACHINE: THE LARGE GREEN ONE WHICH SUPPORTS THE RED PYRAMID.

MAN: *Is there a large block behind a pyramid?*

MACHINE: YES, THREE OF THEM: A LARGE RED ONE, A LARGE GREEN CUBE AND THE BLUE ONE.

MAN: *Put a small one onto the green cube which supports a pyramid.*

MACHINE: OK.

This example illustrates the magnitude of the task insofar as the requirements of computer memory in AI work on natural language in dialog are enormous.

The example also shows that what is to be processed is language as *understanding* so that understanding may be tested as appropriate behavior. Appropriateness is judged as proper responses in language and action resulting from dialog between a machine and a human.

NATURAL-LANGUAGE PROCESSING

There is no contradiction . . . between the thesis that a human being possesses, at birth, a competence for acquiring and using language and the thesis that language is the most artificial, hence also the most human of all constructions. (Simon 1969:52)

This assertion rests on the idea that competence is a kind of "inner environment" which limits "the kinds of information processing" within the capability of humans. Language structure reveals these limits which are common to all humans.

The artificiality assertion holds that

> the limits on adaptation, in possible languages, imposed on the inner environment are very broad limits on organization, not very specific limits on syntax. Moreover, according to the thesis, they are limits imposed not only on language but also on every other mode of representing internally experience received through stimuli from outside. (Simon 1969:52)

AI research in natural-language processing rests on an assumption that linguistic competence, as the ability to produce and understand sentences, depends "on some characteristics of the central nervous system which are common to all languages *but also essential to other aspects of human thinking besides speech and listening*" (emphasis mine) (Simon 1969: 48). AI research sees language as related to thought and therefore values natural-language processing as extremely important in simulating thought (intelligence).

Of paramount importance to natural-language processors is the development of "an adequate semantics to complement syntax" (1969:49). To this end, some research is on developing *memory structures*. The idea is that memory is associative. The associations are like computer list structures which are "sorts of generalizations about human thinking." One hypothesis is that "memory is an organization of list structures (lists whose components can also be lists), which include descriptive components (two-termed relations) and short (three-element or four-element) component lists." (Simon 1969:46) Simon contends that if memory is formally organized like this, then visual, auditory, and even "symbolic" material may all be explained as storable.

One program developed by Laurent Siklossy, an AI researcher, operates on pictures that have been transformed into list structures as the memory internal representation of the pictures. This program is geared to process appropriate natural language sentences saying what is depicted in the pictures.

Different researchers suggest various models of memory

structure, all of which have the common goal of understanding human cognitive processes in general. Rumelhart and Levin (1975:179) developed a language comprehension system called VERBWORLD in which "comprehension of a sentence or answering of a question proceeds in a uniform manner . . . [,and] the intelligence of the system is distributed throughout the semantic network base." In the VERBWORLD system, the key notion is that of the *semantically primitive predicate* which underlies verb meanings. The primitives are stative, change, causative, and actional (Rumelhart and Norman, 1975:47), each being associated with a different aspect of verb meaning so that all verbs seem to have at least one, and a single verb may contain all of them.

The primitive predicates are used to build a network structure for sentence comprehension. The basic premise of the system is that

> . . . information within human memory can be represented by means of what we call an *active structural network*. The word "active" means that the structures are both data and process. The knowledge structures are represented by a labeled, connected network or graph that consists of a set of *nodes* interconnected by a set of *relations* . . . These relations are used by the memory system to encode logical or semantic associations among nodes. (Rumelhart and Norman 1975:36)

The processing of natural language is accomplished through procedural definitions of the predicate terms in the sentence. Therefore, the system understands *John gave Fido to Mary* by treating it as a call to the procedure *give,* with the concepts for *John, Mary,* and *Fido* justifying the procedure. Comprehension of the sentence results by evaluating the procedure.

The comprehension process in the VERBWORLD system is as follows.

1. Input sentence is divided into a SURFACE PROPOSITION (that is, into its predicate name followed by its arguments).

2. The SURFACE PROPOSITION is converted into its underlying semantic structure.

3. The underlying semantic structure is compared with previously stored information in order to integrate the new information from the input sentence.

4. The appropriate contextual information for comprehending the sentence is retrieved.
a. This is done through processes of verification and information retrieval carried out by the primitive predicates.

> The essence of the VERBWORLD verification process is to extend the capabilities of the primitive predicates so that they carry out a search for matching information in memory before they build new structures. The new function of the primitives is to try to find a structure already stored in memory that matches the structure the primitive would build. If the primitive finds a match, no new structure is built. If the primitive does not find the structure, it builds it in memory. (Rumelhart and Levin 1975:188–89)

The approach used in VERBWORLD in the area of natural-language processing in AI stresses representation of natural language rather than processing. This indicates a trend in AI from processing per se in the belief that "The study of processing structure cannot really be separated from the study of representational structure" (Norman and Rumelhart, 1975: epilogue, p. 408). In the opinion of the VERBWORLD group, many scholars in the related disciplines of linguistics, artificial intelligence, and psychology may be creating a new field: *cognitive science.*

Perhaps linguistic theory as conceived in these pages is really a part of cognitive science in its concern for underlying structures and processes, while language description remains in the area of traditional science and its concern with the observable and testable. Cognitive science, it is suggested, combines natural language study, AI, and, cognitive psychological research.

Summary

Beginning as a unified attempt to describe languages in order to show how they (and perhaps also their speakers) are related, linguistics has developed so that two fields thrive where one began. There are some indications that the two fields of linguistic inquiry may eventually be unified. Such a science of the study of language, however, will attempt to make explicit the structure of language as knowledge both acquired and used.

We have seen, too, that there is an abundance of problems enroute from the early descriptivist unified goal to this newer type of unified goal of linguistic science. Many of these problems have existed since the earliest days of linguistic science. For example, no theory of knowledge or of description to date has a satisfactory way of dealing with the intent behind a speaker's utterance, sentence, or message. Likewise, there is no explanation of why humans speak, use sentences, and communicate. By using various definitions of language, scholars have made inroads in describing their particular targeted subject matters.

Descriptivists have made headway in the analysis of *speech* as composed of hierarchically structured levels of sound and grammatical meaning. *Structuralists* have made headway in the analysis of the system *(langue)* underlying a particular language as being composed of bundles of features of sound and grammatical meaning related to each other by a series of statable oppositions between and among features. *Transformationalists* have made headway in the analysis of the *knowledge* all humans have which enables them to acquire language *(competence)*. This knowledge is envisioned as a structure which can be represented by a formal model composed of rules of sound features as linked to rules of semantic interpretation. The sets of rules in the phonological and semantic components are mediated by the syntactic component of grammar. These interrelated components comprise a theory of language modeled as one of the cognitive structures humans have.

Many scholars of language believe that since 1957 the field of linguistics has undergone a revolution; however, the result of this "revolution" has not been to supplant the old linguistics with a new one. Rather, since 1957 linguistic theory as introduced by Chomsky's writings and language description *(the* linguistics up to 1957) have become two areas of inquiry instead of one. Furthermore, an ultimate reunification is possible. Had a *true* revolution occurred that eventuality would have been eclipsed.

One of the more interesting by-products of twentieth-century developments in the scientific study of language is that communication has become the target of much of the description being done. To describe speech elicited from an informant no longer seems sufficient if progress is to be achieved in describing the intent or content of speech in language as well as its expression. Thus, studies in sociolinguistics, studies of animal language, efforts at machine translation plus stratificational and tagmemic analysis of speech and text data now entail looking at messages communicated (in terms of input and output, and in terms of measures of appropriateness and effectiveness). This communicational view is advanced in an effort to be able to describe the content side of linguistic behavior.

In the nonbehavior-oriented approach to language, the main post-1957 orientation appears to be in the focus on attempting to delimit the structure of knowledge. Both TG linguists and natural-language processing experts in the field of artificial intelligence regard language as reason (knowledge) rather than as behavior. They believe that if language is rational knowledge expressed by mental processes, then models of language as a mental process will open the door to the understanding of other cognitive structures as well.

In the 1970s, then, language as an object of scientific inquiry is both thought and behavior. It is actively being researched as both by theorists and descriptivists. When language as thought and language as behavior are each understood, it may be possible to arrive again at a unified science of language, whether as competence and performance or as messages and intent/content. Linguistics in the 1970s as both linguistic theory and language description resembles many of the "harder" sciences. This dual nature of science exists in physics as deductive theory and experimental physics. Language description, in a sense, is analogous to experimental physics with descriptive linguistics an overt deductive theory. Where the physicist ponders the nature of the universe, the linguist ponders the nature of language. The theory of relativity seeks to describe the laws reality obeys and to model its structure. Similarly, the theory of linguistic competence seeks to describe the laws language obeys and to model its structure. Like experiments in physics, language descriptions serve to check proposed models of the phenomena at issue. Thus, these areas of empirical research serve to check the assertions made by reality and competence models respectively. Where theory may describe the laws, a phenomenon (for example, reality, linguistic competence) obeys, questions linger in linguistics (and in physics) regarding the "inner nature of things." The linguistic theorist or language describer still is stymied by the "inner nature" of their analytical objects. For physics, it is felt that this inner nature of things "is left to the philosopher, who says a great deal, but in the end we never appear to be much, if any, the better for it." (Durell 1926:143) For language, it is this "inner nature" of things that continues to motivate the linguist. Linguistic theorists *are* philosophers and, for the most part, linguists.

Unlike physicists in the 1920s, they believe that we will be the better for what they as philosophers *and* linguists have to say. Once the "philosophical" was opposed to the "scientific"; today there is considered to be no incompatibility. In fact, Chomsky (1975:227) believes that both rationalists and empiricist ideas need to be considered today as they interrelate because

> . . . we are under no compulsion to adhere strictly to one or the other framework . . . But I do think that by sharpening these opposed conceptions and exploring them in the light of empirical research, we can move towards a solution to problems that can now sensibly be posed with regard to the nature and acquisition of cognitive structures.

For Thought and Discussion

1. We saw that in some instances the expectations of the meaning of a sentence in English uttered by a speaker of BEV are not met by a hearer who speaks a different English dialect. Think of other examples (hypothetical, if necessary) where the communication process is hindered because a rule of one's dialect is missing in another's dialect. What might some consequences be if the hearer were a White SE-speaking teacher in an urban school and the speaker a Black BEV-speaking pupil?
2. When Sarah, your pet dog, "speaks" at your command, is she really speaking, employing utterances, or communicating? If you feel she is doing any of these things, explain whether what

Sarah does is use elements of speech, sentences, or messages and how this "use" can be described. If Sarah, in your opinion, does none of these things, what does she do? Is she better at "language-ing" than Fido, Washoe, and others? Compare Sarah's act with what you think it is that chimps are doing.

3. Why would AI researchers feel that robots which are built to obey spoken commands have describable linguistic competence while chimps that obey spoken commands do not? Think of ways that teaching language to a chimpanzee and writing programs to control robots are projects of the same kind. Then, think of how the tasks differ.

4. Distinguish the following terms (contrasted throughout this book both implicitly and explicitly) so that you understand their differences and why the distinctions have been made for the study of language.

a. competence and performance
b. competence and *langue*
c. *langue* and *parole*
d. induction and deduction
e. speech and communication
f. deep structure and surface structure
g. empiricism and rationalism
h. competence and communicative competence
i. categorical rules and variable rules
j. language acquisition and language learning
k. *Langue* and speech community

5. For each distinction made in your answer to the previous question, cite the approach(es) to linguistic theory or language description where the distinction is important and say why it is important.

For example, for i you might state that categorical rules are rules expressing a general linguistic regularity in language and that rules of this type are the usual rule in a competence model, such as $S \rightarrow (Q) NP + VP$, while variable rules are proposed by sociolinguists to account for the likelihood of a particular instance of linquistic performance to occur in speakers of particular social, economic, or geographical groups in particular contents. For example, speakers of English may drop final /r/s on words which occur before other words starting with consonants (for example, [ka: + pɔ:t] for *carport*). The likelihood that a speaker will do this depends on where the speaker lives and to what socioeconomic class the speaker belongs. Thus, the rule for deleting final /r/s in English is a variable rule.

6. Try to come up with a definition of language. To help with this, check the indexes of as many textbooks on introductory or intermediate linguistics as you can find. Do linguists usually define language? If they do, what is the most common definition? If you find that linguists tend not to define language, what do they define as their subject matter?

For comparison, look at the situation in some of the other social sciences. Do anthropologists define culture? Do sociologists define society? What do political scientists have to say about politics?

7. What do you think of the concept of sociolinguistics seen as the sociology of language in the sense espoused by the ethnography of speaking? Do you feel that language is part of society? Or, is society part of language? Would it be possible and/or desirable to develop a science of society based on a linguistic model? What kinds of ideas does such a suggestion bring to your mind? Imagine what form such a development might take. Would you consider that theory or description would be the best approach? What would be or could be the goal of such a linguistics of society?

8. Chomsky discusses language as a cognitive structure, suggesting that a formal model of the acquisition of the knowledge humans have which allows them to acquire this structure is a theory of language. Suppose that other cognitive structures can also be modeled this way. What might some of these be? Think of what a theory of these structures might look like based on an analogy with Chomsky's ideas.

Next, suppose that religion is a cognitive structure—like language is thought to be—and extend the analogy as far as you can.

9. Where in the previous question you were asked to compare religion and language as cognitive structures, now consider other possible models of describing religion. In this answer draw analogies with the proposals for language description discussed in Chapters Two, Four, and Five, using religion rather than language as the descriptive object.

10. What do you think a unified linguistics ought to describe? What should such a scientific field account for in the world? Do you believe that linguistics is on its way to being a unified science? Or, do you believe that linguistic theory and language description are becoming more separated and developing as independent fields on their own? Give reasons for your answer. How do you think either unification or diversification will be accomplished?

Bibliography

Abercrombie, David. *Elements of General Phonetics*. Chicago: 1967, Aldine Publishing Company.

Algeo, John. *Stratificational Grammar*. In Makkai and Lockwood, eds. 1973, pp. 4–11, reprinted from *Journal of English Linguistics*. An earlier version appeared in the *South Atlantic Bulletin* 23 (1968):2; 1–4.

———. Tagmemics: A Brief Overview. in Brend, ed., 1974, pp. 1–10. Reprinted from *Journal of English Linguistics* 4 (1970):1–6.

Allen, J. P. B., and Paul Van Buren. *Chomsky: Selected Readings*. New York: 1971, Oxford University Press.

Altmann, S. A. Primates. In Sebeok, ed. 1968.

Bach, Emmon. *An Introduction to Transformational Grammars*. New York: 1964, Holt, Rinehart and Winston.

———. *Syntactic Theory*. New York: 1974, Holt, Rinehart and Winston.

———and Robert T. Harms, eds. *Universals in Linguistic Theory*. New York: 1968, Holt, Rinehart and Winston.

Bauman, Richard, and Joel Sherzer, eds. *Explorations in the Ethnography of Speaking*. New York: 1974, Cambridge University Press.

Bloomfield, Leonard. *Language*. New York: 1933, Henry Holt Company.

Boas, Franz. *Handbook of American Indian Languages*. Bureau of American Ethnology Bulletin No. 40. Washington: 1911, Goverment Printing Office.

Bolinger, Dwight. *Aspects of Language*. New York: 1968, Harcourt, Brace, and World.

———. *Aspects of Language*. 2d ed. New York: 1975, Harcourt Brace Jovanovich.

Booth, T. L. *Sequential Machines and Automata Theory*. New York: 1967, John Wiley and Sons.

Brend, Ruth M., ed. *Advances in Tagmemics*. New York: 1974, North-Holland Publishing Company. Linguistic Series, Vol. 9.

Brown, Roger. *A First Language: The Early Stages*. Cambridge, Mass.: 1973, Harvard University Press.

———. The Development of Language in Children. In Miller, ed., 1973, pp. 107–16.

Chomsky, Noam. *Syntactic Structures*. The Hague: 1957, Mouton and Company. (1965 ed).

———. A Transformational Approach to Syntax. 1958, In Hill ed., 1962, pp. 124–58.

———. The Logical Basis of Linguistic Theory in *Proceedings of the 9th International Congress of Linguists*. The Hague: 1964, Mouton and Company.

———. *Aspects of the Theory of Syntax*. Cambridge, Mass.: 1965, MIT Press.

———. *Current Issues in Linguistic Theory*. The Hague: 1966, Mouton and Company.

———. Basic Principles. In Allen and Van Buren, 1971. Reprinted from Reibel and Schane, 1968, where it appeared as "The Current Scene in Linguistics: Present Directions," pp. 3–7.

———. *Language and Mind*. New York: 1972, Harcourt Brace Jovanovich.

———. Some Empirical Issues in the Theory of Transformational Grammars. In Peters, Ed., 1972, pp. 63–130.

———. Introduction. *The Logical Structure of Linguistic Theory*. 1975. New York: 1973, Plenum Publishing Corporation.

———. On the Nature of Language" 1974, In Steven R. Harnad, Horst D. Steklis, and Jane Lancaster, eds., 1976, pp. 46–66.

Clark, Virgina P., Paul A. Eschholz, and Alfred F. Rosa, eds. *Language Introductory Readings*. New York: 1972, St. Martin's Press.

———. *Reflections on Language*. New York: 1975, Pantheon Books.

Cole, M., and Sylvia Scribner. *Culture and Thought: A Psychological Introduction*. New York: 1974, John Wiley and Sons.

Delavenay, E. *An Introduction to Machine Translation*. New York: 1960, Frederick A. Praeger.

DeSaussure, Ferdinand. *Course in General Linguistics*. Translated from the French by Wade Baskin, 1916, Charles Bally and Albert Sechehaye eds. in collaboration with Albert Reidlinger. New York: Philosophical Library, 1959. Published in 1966 as McGraw-Hill paperback.

Devito, Joseph A. *Psycholinguistics*. Indianapolis: 1971, Bobbs-Merrill Company.

Dinneen, Francis P., *An Introduction to General Linguistics*. New

York: 1967, Holt, Rinehart and Winston.

Durell, Clement V. *Readable Relativity*. New York: 1926, Harper and Row, Harper Torchbook, 1960.

Eddington, A. S. *Mathematical Theory of Relativity*. New York: 1960, Cambridge University Press.

Eastman, Carol M. *Aspects of Language and Culture*. Corte Madera, Calif.: 1975, Chandler and Sharp.

Ervin-Tripp, Susan. On Sociolinguistic Rules: Alternation and Co-occurrence. In Gumperz and Hymes, eds., 1972, pp. 213–50.

Farb, Peter. *Word Play*. New York: 1974, Alfred A. Knopf.

Feigenbaum, E. A., and Julian Feldman, eds. *Computers and Thought*. New York: 1963, McGraw-Hill Book Company.

Ferguson, Charles A. On Sociolinguistically Oriented Surveys. *The Linguistic Reporter*. 9(4):1–3, 1966.

Fillmore, Charles. The Case for Case. In Bach and Harms, eds., 1968, pp. 1–88.

———. On Generativity. In Peters, ed., 1972, pp. 1–19.

Fishman, Joshua A., ed. *Readings in the Sociology of Language*. The Hague: 1968, Mouton and Company. New York: Humanities Press.

Fraser, C. Discussion of McNeil. In McNeil, 1966, pp. 115–20.

Fried, V., ed. *The Prague School of Linguistics and Language Teaching*. New York: 1973, Oxford University Press.

Fromkin, Victoria, and Robert Rodman. *An Introduction to Language*. New York: 1974, Holt, Rinehart and Winston.

Garvin, P. L. A Linguistic View of Language Data Processing. In Garvin, ed., 1963, pp. 109–27.

———. *Natural Language and the Computer*. New York: 1963, McGraw-Hill Book Company.

———. The Definitional Model of Language. In Garvin, ed., 1963, pp. 3–22.

———. *On Machine Translation*. The Hague: 1972, Mouton and Company.

Ginsburg, S. *The Mathematical Theory of Context-Free Languages*. New York: 1966, McGraw-Hill Book Company.

Gleason, H. A. *An Introduction to Descriptive Linguistics*. Rev. ed. New York: 1961, Holt, Rinehart and Winston.

Gumperz, John J. Foreword. In Sanches and Blount, eds. 1975, pp. xi–xxi.

———, and Dell Hymes, ed. *Directions in Sociolinguistics: The Ethnography of Communication*. New York: 1972, Holt, Rinehart and Winston.

Hale, A. On the Systematization of Box 4. In Brend, ed., 1974, pp. 55–74.

Harnad, Steven R., Horst D. Steklis, and Jane Lancaster eds. *Origins and Evolution of Language and Speech*. Annals of the New York Academic of Sciences, Vol. 280, 1976.

Harris, Zellig. Simultaneous Components in Phonology. *Language* 20:181–205, 1944. Also in Joos, ed., 1963, 124–38.

———. *Structural Linguistics*. Chicago: 1951, University of Chicago Press.

———. Distribution Structure. 1954, *Word* 10, nos. 2–3: 146–62.

———. Co-occurrence and Transformations in Linguistic Structure. 1957, *Language* 33, 3: 283–340.

Harrison, Charles. Haida Grammar. 1895, *Proceedings and Transactions of the Royal Society of Canada* I(2) (section 2): 123–226.

Haugen, Einar, Directions in Modern Linguistics, 1951, *Language* 27: 211–22 also in Joos, ed. 1963, pp. 357–78.

Hays, David. Research Procedures in Machine Translation. In Garvin, ed., 1963, pp. 183–214.

Hill, Archibald, ed. *Proceedings* of the Third Texas Conference on Problems of Linguistic Analysis in English. Austin: 1962, University of Texas Press.

Hjelmslev, L. *Prolegomena to a Theory of Language*. Translated by Francis J. Whitfield. Madison: 1961, University of Wisconsin Press.

Hockett, Charles. Two Models of Grammatical Description. 1954, *Word* 10:210–31. Also in Joos, ed., 1963, pp. 386–99.

———. *A Course in Modern Linguistics*. New York: 1958, Macmillan Company.

Hunt, Earl. *Artificial Intelligence*. New York: 1975, Academic Press.

Hymes, Dell. Models of the Interaction of Language and Social Life. In Gumperz and Hymes, eds., 1972, pp. 35–71.

———. Ways of Speaking. In Bauman and Sherzer, eds., 1974, pp. 433–51.

Jakobson, Roman, and Morris Halle. *Fundamentals of Language*. The Hague: 1956, Mouton and Company.

Joos, Martin. Acoustic Phonetics. Language Monograph no. 23 Supplement to *Language* 24:2, 1948, (April–June).

———. ed. *Readings in Linguistics*. Washington: 1963, ACLS.

Klima, E., and Ursula Bellugi. Teaching Apes to Communicate. In Miller, ed., 1973, pp. 95–106.

Kucera, Henry "Computers in Language Analysis and in Lexicography" From the *American Heritage Dictionary of the English Language*. New York: 1969, 1970, 1971, American Heritage Publishing Company. Chap. 5 (of Part III) in Clark, Eschholz, and Rosa, 1972, pp. 254–59.

Labov, William. *The Social Stratification of English in New York*

City. Washington: 1966, Center for Applied Linguistics.

————. *Sociolinguistic Patterns*. Philadelphia: 1972, University of Pennsylvania Press.

Lamb, Sydney. *Outline of Stratificational Grammar*. Washington: 1966, Georgetown University Press.

————. The Crooked Path of Progress in Cognitive Linguistics. In Richard J. O'Brien, ed., 1971, pp. 99–124.

Langacker, Ronald. *Language and Its Structure*. New York: 1968, Harcourt, Brace and World.

Langness, L. L. *The Study of Culture*. Corte Madera, Calif.: 1974, Chandler and Sharp.

Lehmann, Winfred. *Descriptive Linguistics: An Introduction*. New York: 1972, Random House.

Linden, Eugene. *Apes, Men, and Language*. New York: 1975, Saturday Review Press.

Longacre, Robert E. *Grammar Discovery Procedures*. The Hague: 1964, Mouton and Company.

————. Some Fundamental Insights of Tagmemics. In Brend, ed, 1974, pp. 11–22.

Lyons, John, and R. J. Wales, eds. Psycholinguistics Papers. *Proceedings* of the 1966 Edinburgh Conference. Edinburgh: 1966, Edinburgh University Press.

Makkai, Adam, and David G. Lockwood, eds. *Readings in Stratificational Linguistics*. 1973, University of Alabama Press.

Malmberg, Bertil. *Phonetics*. New York: 1963, Dover Books.

McNeil, David. The Creation of Language by Children. In Lyons and Wales, eds., 1966, pp. 99–132.

Michie, D. *On Machine Intelligence*. Edinburgh: 1974, Edinburgh University Press.

Miller, George A., ed. *Communication Language, and Meaning: Psychological Perspectives*. New York: 1973, Basic Books.

Mounin, G. Language, Communication, Chimpanzees. *Current Anthropology* 17:1976, 1–21.

Nida, Eugene. *Morphology: The Descriptive Analysis of Words*. Rev. ed. Ann Arbor: 1949, University of Michigan Press.

Norman, D., and David E. Rumelhart, eds. *Explorations in Cognition*. San Francisco: 1975, W. H. Freeman and Company.

O'Brien, R. J., ed. *Linguistics: Developments of the Sixties — Viewpoints for the Seventies*. Georgetown University School of Languages and Linguistics, 1971, 22d Annual Roundtable Number 24.

Ortiz, Alejandro and Ernesto Zierer. *Set Theory and Linguistics*. The Hague: 1968, Mouton and Company.

Parret, Herman. *Discussing Language*. The Hague: 1974, Mouton and Company.

Pedersen, Holgar. *The Discovery of Language: Linguistic Science in the Nineteenth Century.* Translated by John Webster Spargo. Bloomington: 1959, Indiana University Press.

Peters, Stanley, ed. *Goals of Linguistic Theory.* Englewood Cliffs, N. J.: 1972, Prentice-Hall.

Pike, Kenneth. *Language in Relation to a Unified Theory of the Structure of Human Behavior,* 3 parts, Glendale (now Santa Ana) Calif. Summer Institute of Linguistics (Part 1, 1954; Part 2, 1955; Part 3, 1960; 2d rev. ed., 1967. The Hague: 1954–1960, Mouton and Company.

———. *Tagmemic and Matrix Linguistics Applied to Selected African Languages.* Norman, Okla.: 1970, Summer Institute of Linguistics.

———. Crucial Questions in the Development of Tagmemics—The Sixties and Seventies. In Brend, ed., 1974. pp. 35–54.

Postal, Paul. *Constituent Structure: A Study of Contemporary Models of Syntactic Description.* Bloomington: 1967, Indiana University Press and the Hague: Mouton and Company. Originally published as Part 2 *IJAL* 30: #1 1964.

———. *Aspects of Phonological Theory.* New York: 1968, Harper and Row.

Pound, Louise. American Euphemisms for Dying, Death, and Burial 1936, In Clark, Eschholz, and Rosa, 1972, pp. 312–19.

Random House Dictionary of the English Language. New York: 1968, Random House.

Reibel, David, and Sanford A. Schane. *Modern Studies in English.* Englewood Cliffs, N.J.: 1969, Prentice-Hall.

Rumelhart, David E., and James A. Levin. A Language Comprehension System. In Norman and Rumelhart, eds., 1975. pp. 179–208.

Rumelhart, David E., and Donald A. Norman. The Active Structural Network. In Norman and Rumelhart, eds., 1975, pp. 36–64.

Sampson, G. *Stratificational Grammar.* The Hague: 1970, Mouton and Company.

Sanches, Mary, and Ben G. Blount, eds. *Sociocultural Dimensions of Language Use.* New York: 1975, Academic Press.

Sankoff, Gillian. A Quantitative Paradigm for the Study of Communicative Competence. In Bauman and Sherzer, eds., 1974, pp. 18–49.

Sapir, Edward, *Language: An Introduction to the Study of Speech* New York: 1921, Harcourt, Brace and Company.

Sebeok, Thomas A., ed. *Animal Communication: Techniques of Study and Results of Research.* Bloomington: 1968, Indiana University Press.

Simon, H. *The Science of the Artificial.* Cambridge, Mass.: 1969, MIT Press.

Southworth, Franklin C., and C. J. Daswani. *Foundations of Linguistics*. New York: 1974, The Free Press.

Troike, Rudolph, The View From the Center: The Future of MT. *The Linguistic Reporter* 1976, 18, 9: p. 2.

Trubetzkoy, N. *Introduction to the Principles of Phonological Descriptions*. The Hague: 1935, Martinus/Nijhoff. As translated in 1968 by L. A. Murray, edited by H. Bluhme.

Vachek, Josef. The Linguistic Theory of the Prague School. In Fried, V., ed., 1972, pp. 10–28.

Wallace, Anthony F. C., and John Atkins. The Meaning of Kinship Terms. *American Anthropologist* 1960, 62:58–80.

Waterhouse, Viola. *The History and Development of Tagmemics.* The Hague: 1974, Mouton and Company.

Webster's Third New International Dictionary. Springfield, Mass: 1961, G. & C Merriam Company,

Webster's New World Dictionary of the American Language. Cleveland: 1964, The World Publishing Company.

Wells, Rulon. Immediate Constituents. In Joos, ed., 1963, pp. 186–207. Reprinted from *Language* 23:81–117 (1947).

Index